CALLING UP

PRAISE FOR *CALLING UP*

"J.P. did a fascinating job creating a storyline that not only keeps you engaged but drives you all throughout to think deeper and challenge yourself to a higher level of coaching. He essentially does what the title reads; calls us up! Great read!"

$\qquad$ –Adam Bradley, Founder and Director of **Lead-Em Up**
$\qquad$ and the of *The Hardwood Hustle* Podcast

"J.P. has woven a compelling tale of a struggling coach and his mentor that highlights many of the issues facing coaches today. The book highlights all the important issues and will help the reader become a better leader and a more influential coach."

$\qquad$ –John O'Sullivan, Founder and CEO of **Changing the Game Project**

"I highly recommend all coaches AND parents read this book! I frantically underlined and scribbled notes as I went. There is so much incredibly important information to help guide and provide a blue print for what it really means to be a leader!"

$\qquad$ –Asia Mape, Founder of **ilovetowatchyouplay.com**

"J.P.'s fable *Calling Up* should be mandatory reading for coaches of all backgrounds. Easy to read, relatable, and full of practical advice—this book will cause you to reflect on your own coaching practices, but even more importantly, will help you have a greater impact those you lead."

–Nate Sanderson, Head Basketball Coach at Linn Marr High School
and **Breakthrough Basketball**

"*Calling Up* brings exactly the kind of message all of us need to hear as coaches. Leading with positivity and authentic care for your athletes will always create better results than fear and authoritarianism. Delivering this message through a relatable character and entertaining story makes the message twice as powerful."

–Pete Jacobson, Founder of **WinSmarter.com** and
Head Wrestling Coach at Edgemont High School

CALLING UP

UP

**Discovering
Your Journey to
Transformational
Leadership**

J. P. NERBUN

NEW YORK

LONDON • NASHVILLE • MELBOURNE • VANCOUVER

CALLING UP

Discovering Your Journey to Transformational Leadership

Published in New York, New York, by Morgan James Publishing. Morgan James is a trademark of Morgan James, LLC. www.MorganJamesPublishing.com

ISBN 9781642793048 paperback
ISBN 9781642793055 eBook
Library of Congress Control Number: 2018911954

Cover Design by:
Rachel Lopez
www.r2cdesign.com

Interior Design by:
Christopher Kirk
www.GFSstudio.com

Morgan James is a proud partner of Habitat for Humanity Peninsula and Greater Williamsburg. Partners in building since 2006.

Get involved today! Visit
MorganJamesPublishing.com/giving-back

For my parents, Ann and Bob, who loved me from the beginning.
For my wife, Melissa, who will love me forever

CONTENTS

ACKNOWLEDGMENTS

Thank you first and foremost to my wife, Melissa Nerbun, who has supported me every step of the way on this journey.

I'm so grateful for my parents, Robert and Ann Nerbun, who instilled in me a passion for life and the desire to become the best version of myself.

Thank you to my great friend John Wilson who has been one of my most consistent believers and supporters in my life.

Thank you to Jamie Gilbert for your guidance and friendship these last few years.

Thank you to all my former assistant coaches, players, and athletic directors. Especially Glen Carr, Francisco Soutoyo, and Matt Pobieglo. Without your support I might have left coaching years ago!

A special shout out to the Men of Iron: Brian Catanella, Dustin Krause, Taylor Edge, Justin Simpkins, and Nate Sanderson.

Thank you to my editor Justin Spizman and publisher Morgan James. You have believed in this project and helped make this book great!

I'm so grateful for all the special friends in my life. I have been blessed with an incredible group of people—all are so unique and different.

To download the Calling Up Coaching Guide PDF,
go to **thriveonchallenge.com**.
The guide provides tools and activities for implementing a
personal and cultural system that can be done while reading
the book or after reading the book.

PART I
SEARCHING FOR CLARITY

Climbing mountains can serve as a great metaphor for life's journey. The story of Part I: Searching for Clarity predominately takes place on a journey up a mountain. The main character, Danny, is searching for clarity of purpose and a process to close the gap from where he is to where he wants to be in life.

Today's culture seems intently concentrated on the problems of the world, and finding clarity within it can be difficult. The first step is to go backward, not forward. This means stepping back to understand where we are and where we want to go. While our main character, Danny, seeks that clarity through his journey up a mountain, we as coaches can find that clarity in a less dramatic way through reading, reflecting, journaling, and mentorship.

I continue to do the reflections and activities in this section—some even daily—because they help me to be mindful of my actions and attitude. This process requires us to continuously step outside of ourselves to reflect on our beliefs, principles, and behaviors.

CHAPTER 1

USED BY YOUR SPORT

Danny sat on a stool in the empty locker room with his head in his hands. A million things seemed to be racing through his head. He had felt the pain of loss before with some ugly seasons, and every loss seemed more agonizing than the last. As a coach, you get used to the ups and downs of your sport. Extreme highs and even deeper lows. The losses were much more sour and the wins sweeter. No matter how many times Danny experienced loss, he just couldn't get used to it. Each loss still felt like an unexpected and unwelcomed experience, like jumping into a freezing cold pool. Loss sucked. Every single time. But this one seemed to cut a little deeper and burn a little more than all the rest.

Four years . . . four years of sacrificing so much, only to have it end like this? They'd won their conference championship just last week. What a feeling of elation, the high of highs. But a humiliating loss in the first round of the state tournament quickly overshadowed that accomplishment.

Danny *knew* his team had the potential to develop into something special this season—maybe even to go all the way to the state championship. But his squad fell apart in the last few minutes of the game. Jayden, their star player, had again lost his cool. But this proved to be costly timing. After picking up his fourth foul, Jayden decided to mouth off to the referees. The usually patient refs called a technical foul on Jayden, which led to two free throws for the other team and possession of the basketball. But maybe even worse was that the technical foul also counted as a personal foul, and Jayden was done for the night. The final moments of his high school career seemed to act as a microcosm for his entire story.

As much of a head case as he was, he was every bit of a talented ball player as well. With Jayden on the bench, the team didn't have a true scorer on the court, and blew a six-point lead. They lost in the last few seconds of the game. While the opposing team stormed the court, Danny and his group of men stood by in dismay, trying to comprehend another season of falling short of their goal to make it to the state title game.

None of the team's seniors shed a tear in the locker room after the game. They didn't even thank their teammates and coaches, or express any emotion other than indifference. They seemed apathetic to the situation. Danny, who had spent the last four years pouring everything he had into these young men, felt like he was hugging corpses as he thanked them for their hard work and told them he loved them.

Finally alone and capable of fully comprehending his present circumstances, Danny sat on one of the locker room stools and looked around him at the trash littered everywhere, the jerseys hanging from the lockers, and the random shoes scattered across the floor. Normally, he would have called the team back into the locker room and lectured them about respecting their facilities—even if his admonitions were trite—but he realized he had failed if he hadn't made his point by now.

A failure . . . Yes, that is what he felt he was in his own mind. Even after the conference championship win the week before, he couldn't help but remember how, for the past two years, his team had consistently fallen short of their goals. One win does not erase the pain of past defeats; he understood that now.

The confusing part was that Danny wasn't even that upset with how abruptly the season had ended. For every good moment with these boys, there seemed to be ten that were completely devastating.

Every season, Danny recommitted himself to developing an even greater sense of personal character, and doing things the right way. Early in his coaching career, he believed the myth that sports build character. However, he had listened to a talk from a coach named Joe Ehrmann, who had discussed the "sports build character" myth. Joe said, "They can, and they should. Indeed, sports may be the perfect venue in which to build character. But sports don't build character unless a coach possesses character and intentionally teaches it."

This singular statement inspired Danny to build strong young men and make a difference in their lives. To do that, Danny attempted to hold them accountable to really high standards. In spite of his best efforts, they only seemed to backfire. The more he tried to *make* them better men, the more his players seemed to fight him, and the weaker his relationships grew with the young men whom he had once felt liked him enough to enroll at Washington Prep. As the season progressed, Danny struggled to find the emotional energy he needed to motivate the players to live up to the high standards he had set forth. It just seemed like diminished returns, and he was recognizing no return on his investment. He had definitely run out of the energy it took to hold them accountable. He was burned out and felt lost, as if he were navigating treacherous waters in a small and poorly built boat.

At one point in the most recent season, he even suspended Jayden for three games and threatened to kick him off the team. Suspending Jayden gave Danny a brief sense of relief, as he knew he was strong enough to bench his top player and face the critics. His decision caught the attention of so many people in the city. However, Jayden's parents—who had supported Danny for years—were suddenly not in his corner anymore. According to them, it would be Danny's fault if Jayden lost his scholarship offers.

This made Danny think about the parents of all his players. He dreaded facing them after any loss, much less this one. Nothing he did was ever good enough for them. He was always "too hard on the boys," even when the team clearly showed a lack of discipline. If they were losing, it was always due to a lack of good coaching, not a lack of talent or effort. If they won games, they didn't win by enough, or their son didn't play enough or score enough. It was a lose/lose for Danny. He never got a "thank you" after a practice or game. Instead, he often received a phone call or a text, because they would rarely have the courage to make those comments to his face. He was their punching bag and their scapegoat.

Danny had tried to forge positive relationships with the parents, encouraging team get-togethers with the families after games, or inviting them to travel to tournaments with the team. But they weren't interested in getting to know the other families. They were too focused on making sure their sons received the attention they "deserved." He knew they didn't feel he was the right man for the job, that they resented him and constantly compared him to the other coaches in the school, who consistently won games and secured athletic scholarships for their players. However, the other coaches' scholarship players barely managed a 2.0 GPA. They rarely finished college, usually flunking out or getting expelled. But who was Danny to point that out to his team's parents?

With all this at the front of his mind, he would still have to step outside that locker room, no matter how terrified he felt about doing so. He knew he'd be met with disapproving looks and possibly a few nasty comments on the other side of that door. He wished he could somehow morph into someone else, so he could escape their forthcoming judgment. Danny didn't want praise or a high-five, he just wanted something as simple as a "thank you."

He felt unappreciated and disrespected, like a complete and total failure. He wanted to quit and be done with it all. It just wasn't worth it anymore. Danny felt like he was constantly caught in a lose/lose proposition. If he won, it wasn't good enough. And if he lost, it was unforgivable. Boy was he tired of losing. The ungrateful and critical parents that watched his every move and decision were exhausting. Then there were the lazy and entitled players who didn't seem to care at all.

Danny was part of a sports culture that valued three things above all else: winning, notoriety, and most of all, money. He wanted something more for the young men who played for him, but he had begun to believe that was nothing more than a pipe dream and simply impossible.

It didn't take but a few hours for Danny to start facing his after-season demons. They reared their ugly heads even earlier this year. He hadn't even made it out of the locker room. But there they were, questioning his very purpose and desire to continue coaching. It just hurt too much—the ups and downs, the unbelievable expectations, and the feeling of aloneness while still being surrounded by dozens of coaches and basketball players.

Next year, if I come back, I will prove to all the people who doubt me that they are wrong. I'm a good coach! I can win! I can build a successful team.

As that thought bounced around in his head, he finally gathered the courage to stand up and walk out that door. As he walked through the gymnasium, he noticed a few straggling players and their families. Cold stares fell upon him, and in response Danny's head fell to the floor.

Typically, his assistants would stay after the game and remain by his side to shield him from approaching parents. But tonight, they had already headed out to the bar. Danny had wanted a few moments alone before he followed suit.

As he walked through the gym, he saw his athletic director, Bill, who was meticulously supervising the gym cleanup. Danny decided to stop by and thank him for his support during the season. Bill had been his rock, a constant source of support, and Danny knew he was lucky to have a friend who supported him like Bill. It was a rare thing, especially in this line of work.

Bill looked up and said, "I know what you're thinking, Danny, but don't. You have done the best with what you know this season. Your value comes from who you are as a person, not your past accomplishments, performance, or even your potential."

With his head down, Danny somberly responded, "I know, Bill, but it's just not good enough. We could have been so much better. We could have gone to the state championship this season. I have failed miserably."

Bill struggled to stay patient. "Danny, when will it be enough for you? Nothing will ever be enough if you find your value in the performance of your team and the scoreboard at the end of the game. Don't make the mistake so many coaches make today: sacrificing their principles and character to climb the ladder . . . to win it all. They all eventually realize they were climbing the wrong ladder and were being used by their sport instead of using their sport to make a positive impact on the world."

Danny pretended to be listening but was only thinking of how few people saw things the way Bill saw them. Bill lived in a different world than most of his counterparts. Even if Bill was right, Danny had still failed to make a difference.

"You think I made a difference in these kids' lives? They are selfish, entitled, and lack mental toughness. Just look at how Jayden finished the game tonight. Pretty much sums up his career and my inability to teach him anything on or off the court. Four years with a player and that's still happening? That's on me! I couldn't reach him. I couldn't make a difference."

Bill paused for a second, as if to let Danny's point set in. "Our sporting culture makes it incredibly difficult for coaches like yourself to try to do what you attempted this season. You tried to use sports to build men of character. To build personal strengths like honesty, self-control, and empathy." As Bill said this, he looked up at Danny and put his hand on his shoulder. "Nobody can do it all, but you have done something. You have done your best. You have sacrificed and invested to help others, and that's where you need to find your value. Until you find your value in the person you are, rather than your achievements, you won't scratch the surface of your potential as a coach and a leader. As a coach, you will almost certainly face a great deal of problems, challenges, and issues. But great coaches are not created in times of victory or during winning streaks, they are forged from the pain of the loss, the struggle of bouncing back, and keeping morale high when the odds are stacked against them."

Reflect and write: What are the problems, challenges, and issues you face as a leader?

Danny thanked Bill. He just wished he could believe him.

As Danny walked to his car, he started to think about his family. Two children and a patient wife awaited him at home. He was a lucky man but felt conflicted in his personal and professional responsibilities. They always seemed to come at the cost of one another. They didn't co-exist, they co-conflicted. He missed his family so much during the season, and his children were not getting any younger. Early mornings and late evenings kept him from his kids nearly every day of the week. He was missing some amazing moments with his family, and for what? To put up with the ungrateful and selfish players and parents? That just didn't sit right with Danny.

Danny eventually made it to his car, and as he carefully placed his key into the ignition, he felt his phone vibrate in his pocket. He grabbed it and focused on the small but bright screen. A text appeared on his phone from Richard, the school principal. As he read the text, his heart nearly stopped. He knew Richard was unhappy with the team's performance, but he didn't realize he was *this* unhappy. The text read: *Disappointing and tough loss tonight. We expect more at Washington Prep. As much as we really like you, Daniel, you have to do better next season.*

Have to? Danny thought. *What does that mean?*

Danny was sick to his stomach and couldn't face going home. Not yet. So, he started his car and headed off to the bar.

CHAPTER 2

HUNGRY FOR CHANGE

Danny had a change of heart on the way to the bar to meet up with his assistant coaches. He couldn't face the usual after-game crowd at the bar. They were always supportive and did a great job of listening, but tonight he was too embarrassed to even face them. He felt he had let them down by falling short of the state championship. Deep down he knew the losses, poor work ethic, and selfish attitudes all fell on him. He wasn't in the mood to listen to anyone making excuses for him.

Looking for a change of scenery on his ride home, he came upon a small hole in the wall called Auggie's Bar. It looked empty with no cars in the parking lot, which was exactly the type of place he wanted to drink tonight. Sure enough, it was just him and a peculiar looking bartender dressed as a monk. He bellied up to the bar, and the bartender offered him only one type of beer, promising Danny it would be the best beer he would ever taste. Danny didn't care at this stage, so long as it numbed the pain. When the beer finally arrived, Danny was happy to find the bartender wasn't lying. It was the most incredible beer ever!

Auggie was the name of the bartender. Danny could see that on his nametag, and he seemed a pleasant fellow with a warm smile. Danny really wasn't in the mood for talking, but after a few beers, he couldn't help but answer Auggie's various questions.

"What brings you in here tonight?"

11

Danny barely lifted his head to respond. "I'm the basketball coach at Washington Prep. Well, I *hope* I'm still the coach . . . or maybe I don't really care anymore. Anyway, I usually head out with my assistant coaches after a game, but our season just ended, and I don't feel like talking to anybody at this stage, so I came here to drink in silence."

Auggie said, "Only one team gets to finish their season with a win, but that math doesn't make it any easier for all the teams that have sacrificed so much all season long. I'm sorry you're upset, and that the season didn't end the way you had hoped." As Auggie said this, Danny thought about how, years ago, he had set the goal to win a state championship but had yet to even win one game in the state tournament. He had not even come close to achieving his goal.

Danny reluctantly looked up, unsure how much he wanted to share with the smiling bartender dressed as a monk. "Some days . . . well, *most* days, I wish I had a much simpler job. I thought all I wanted to be was a basketball coach, but at this stage, I'm so tired of what my job has become. I'm constantly inundated with people's problems. Kids these days don't work hard, are unwilling to sacrifice for others, have a bad attitude, and aren't all that grateful—and all their parents do is coddle them and tell them how great they are. I thought I was going to be a coach for the rest of my life, but at this stage, I'm not sure if I will last even another season! I have failed to achieve nearly every goal I set when I started this job."

"Well, why did you start coaching in the first place?"

"When I started fifteen years ago, I felt I was meant to be a coach. It seemed perfect for me, so I changed more than just my career. I changed a lot about my life to be a coach. I loved teaching kids basketball. As cliché as it sounds, I felt I was making a difference in their lives."

"So, has your 'why' changed?"

Danny paused and pondered whether his "why" had really changed. He still wanted to make a difference in their lives and he wanted to do things the right way. Danny slowly stuttered out a response. "No, I still want to make a difference, but I don't think I'm able anymore. I'm not sure if it is this new generation, the sporting culture, the parents, or that I just suck as a coach."

Auggie seemed able to look right through Danny. He knew Danny wasn't sure of his answer. "Were those goals you set a few years ago really about making a difference in people's lives? Or were they about personal achievement? Think about whether they are really necessary to help you live your 'why' every day. Sometimes what you think the problem is, is really not the problem in the first place."

Danny felt very uncomfortable with his answer. He knew it was true, but he didn't want to admit it, not even to himself. Still, he appreciated the message. "Thanks, Auggie." He paused and then, laughing, half-jokingly asked, "Hey, you want to give me a job? The life of a bartender has to be a lot simpler than the life of a basketball coach. I could sure use a break."

Smiling, Auggie asked, "Is that really what you want to do?"

"I just know I want to be happy and coaching doesn't make me happy anymore because it's filled with stress and mounting problems."

Auggie sighed. "Danny, life is full of challenges and human suffering. You don't find happiness by running from your mounting problems, but by *surmounting* your problems. When you try to escape negative experiences, you will only grow weaker and your problems will only grow stronger until they have more control over you. Avoiding challenges is a challenge in itself. You cannot escape the struggle. I can see great pain in your life. It is clearly tearing you up. People have hurt you and let you down, even after you have sacrificed so much for them. It can be a painful experience when we love others and they use us for their own personal gain. But avoiding this pain will only be destructive."

Danny knew exactly the pain Auggie referenced. He'd spent thousands of hours in the gym training and pushing the young men he coached. He'd given up time with his family and chose a profession in which he would always struggle financially. Instead of being thankful, the kids had walked out on him. The parents had cursed him, talked about him behind his back, and some had even tried to get him fired.

Auggie started to pour him another beer while Danny wondered how this bartender knew so much about what he was experiencing. "No disrespect, Auggie, but how does a bartender know so much about pain? All you have to do is pour people drinks."

"Grass always looks greener on the other side, right?" Danny nodded, knowing this to be true. "But I serve more than drinks. Bartending is my passion, but my purpose is serving others. In my vocation as a person who tends bar, I also serve my clientele by listening. And I can help when I listen. How ironic it is that in the last century, the quality of life in this country has only grown higher and higher, but people only seem to suffer from greater and greater depression, anxiety, and unhappiness? People's search for happiness only sends them to the wrong places, looking for more and more things to fill the void in their lives. So, you think serving in my capacity has less problems than your job as a coach?"

"Absolutely!" Danny replied.

"Mark Manson, a man with a lot of problems in his own life, once said, 'Life is essentially an endless series of problems. The solution to one problem is merely the creation of another.'[1] Even the truly successful people in life—the ones who have scraped and worked their way to the top—they don't have fewer problems! They are just more resilient and determined not to let those problems define their lives. Your problem isn't what you think it is! Your problem is actually your thought process, your paradigm. You are continuously trying to treat the symptoms, not the disease. You have to seek a change of being. You see, problems offer opportunities to grow, to love, and to serve others."

Danny grew frustrated. "Well, that's easy for you to say, but the reality is I have failed myself and everyone around me. My players aren't happy with me. Their parents aren't happy with me. And now the administration of our school isn't happy with me, or my winning percentage. I'll surely get fired if I don't win next year."

---

1   *The Subtle Art of Not Giving a F*ck: A Counterintuitive Approach to Living a Good Life* by Mark Manson

Auggie took a pen and scribbled three words on a beer mat then passed the mat to Danny. Danny looked down at the beer mat, puzzled by what he read:

Condition
Circumstance
Being

Danny then looked up at Auggie, who quickly said, "Although all human motivation arises from a longing for transformation, there are three different types of transformation. When a thirsty man drinks, he transforms his condition. When a poor man hits the lottery, he transforms his circumstance. And when Mr. Scrooge wakes up on Christmas morning an utterly new man, he has experienced a transformation of being. All three types of transformation are necessary. It is only when we try to replace one type of transformation with another that we get into trouble."[2]

Danny sat thinking about what Auggie was trying to tell him, and it started to make sense. "So, I'm really competitive and want to win every game. When I win, I'm transforming my condition."

"Yeah, that's about right. But think about it like this: If you were to classify all your problems, issues, and challenges into these three categories of transformational longing, what would that look like to you? What are some possible solutions to these problems? What are some of the challenges, and how can you overcome them?"

Reflect and write: Classify all your problems, issues, and challenges from Chapter 1 into the three categories of transformational longing: condition, circumstances, and being.

---

2   *Business Secrets of the Trappist Monks: One CEO's Quest for Meaning and Authenticity* by August Turak

"I want players who work harder, parents who appreciate what I do, referees who show me respect, and an administration that actually supports me. If I had all of those things, or maybe even a couple of them, I would transform my circumstances."

"Exactly."

"So, you're suggesting that those things aren't necessarily bad? In the case of keeping my job, while they are necessary, to some extent, what I really need is a transformation of being?"

"Would you be problem-free if you won more games, if players liked you, if parents praised you, and if your administration gave you a blank checkbook at the start of every season? Or would you just have a new set of problems to focus on?"

"Now that you mention it, I'm thinking about the school I coached at before Washington Prep. The kids and parents really liked me, and we were one of the top teams in the league every year. Still, I managed to find problems, even back then in the good old days."

"Exactly. You are constantly raising the bar and expecting more and more from yourself and others. I used to be the same way. I was exhausting to work for and live with! I lost a job I'd held for twelve years and nearly lost my marriage of twenty-one years in the process. I worked hard to change my circumstances. But when that failed, I looked for an easier change—a change of my condition. Popping painkillers was easy; a lot easier than doing what was necessary to experience a transformation of being. I turned it around, stopped trying to substitute one change for another, and started to rethink and retrain the man I became."

"I don't even know what that means, and I'm pretty sure life isn't supposed to be that hard or complicated! Retrain who we are *becoming?*" Danny echoed.

"Yes! We all need a mission in our life. We need to arm ourselves with the principles and disciplines necessary to live out that mission, and then we need to train ourselves to do battle in the world, living by those principles no matter how our circumstances change, what problems arise, or how we are feeling in the moment."

"I need a mission? Something like 'save the world?' I'm no superhero or saint, and I never will be."

Auggie chuckled. "No, you don't need to save anyone. In fact, too many coaches get their high from saving the people they are coaching. In the process, they lose themselves and their family. We need to help, love, and serve others because it is the right thing to do, not because it improves our approval rating and makes us feel better. Great coaches, teachers, and leaders don't save people; they empower them to help themselves and solve their own problems. It's okay to want to be appreciated; that's natural. But it's unhealthy to want to be *needed*. You know any coaches who think they are saviors?"

Danny knew exactly the type of coach Auggie was talking about. Many of the coaches in his school used social media to constantly praise what they did for their players. They loved to talk about how they saved them from a horrible situation or were the reason they turned their life around and constantly bragged about how many athletic scholarships they had gotten for their players.

"Yes, I know a few too many. The fans think they are just the absolute best and few see the truth: that the coach saves them from the consequences of their actions far too many times in their sport, school, and even with the law. And their lives fall apart when those players move on because they haven't been equipped to live with the consequences of their actions."

Auggie was impressed by how quickly Danny caught on, as well as his insights into the sporting culture. "Exactly! As a servant leader, you serve the needs of the people you lead. They are not there to fulfill your needs. Your mission as a coach needs to be about serving, not saving."

"I want to agree with what you're saying, but I have to win if I want to keep my job next year, no matter how hard or successful I'm in my service to others."

Auggie said, "I'm not arguing that winning doesn't matter, just that having a mission and the opportunity to be transformed through that mission matter much more."

Danny finished his last beer and put on his coat. "Well, that all sounds really nice and idealistic, but I don't believe that any coach can really operate that way. I need to get home to my family now, who I will have to figure out a way to feed in a year's time unless I'm able to win."

Auggie shook Danny's hand and laughed as he said, "If you build it, they will come—you ever watch *Field of Dreams*?"

"Yeah, it's not my favorite. I'm not a baseball guy and never really understood it."

"Everyone longs for the opportunity to be transformed through something greater than themselves, whether they know it or not. A transformational team that is committed to serving each other . . . build it."

Danny thought that sounded like the type of pie-in-the-sky advice that seemed practical but hardly implementable. As he digested the seemingly unhelpful guidance, Auggie started again.

"Danny, it starts with you experiencing that transformation of being—I suggest you start by taking the journey I took so many years ago."

"What journey is that?"

"The journey up Clearview Mountain!"

CHAPTER 3

PREPARE FOR THE JOURNEY

Danny felt completely lost.

He looked around him for anything that could offer a sign of where to head next, but there was nothing. Here he was, on the first day of his journey, completely stranded in the middle of nowhere on some foolish expedition to climb Clearview Mountain. With no cell service and nobody around, he started to think everyone had been right in the first place.

The week after their last game had been a hellacious one, with rumors of multiple players saying they wouldn't play basketball next year, and even a group of parents starting a petition to the principal and athletic director to fire him. After meeting with Principal Richard and the athletic director, Bill, he didn't feel much better at all. Richard seemed to almost suggest it might be best if he left at the end of the year. Bill, one of the people whom he trusted the most at the school, suggested he get away for a while and think things over. Completely on edge all week, Danny seemed to only take it out on his wife and two little kids.

"I love you, you know that," his wife, Brownie, had said. "And we understand you are going through a tough time. But we aren't going to be your punching bag. You need to get away and think things over, just like Bill suggested. Something has got to change if you are going to come back and coach next year. We can't go on like this." Brownie was always so empathetic with his struggles, but even she was through with it all.

Change.

Transformation.

Those two words had stuck with him all week long, and now even Brownie had pointed out the importance of a significant change. He knew she wasn't looking for him to lose weight, win more games, or even make more money. Brownie wanted the same transformation Auggie had talked about. A transformation of being.

So, Danny decided to hike up the legendary Clearview Mountain that Auggie had suggested he climb. For a mountain of relatively average height, Clearview was known to be incredibly challenging, especially in the winter months. Never having done much hiking or climbing, his wife and friends had called him foolish, and Brownie had nearly forbidden him to go.

"Well, we don't have any money for me to go rent a place at the beach to sit on the sand, and I don't want that anyway," he had told her. "I need to stretch myself and challenge myself. I will be okay!"

So, he loaded up the car full of camping gear and food and set off on the four-hour drive to the base of the mountain. As he got to the mountain around mid-morning, he threw on his backpack and off he went. How hard could it be, right? Just climb straight up!

Well, Danny quickly realized it was more difficult than just that. He ended up navigating off course to avoid the most difficult parts of the mountain. He was completely lost within two hours of starting his expedition, had no cell service, and couldn't find a soul in site.

What a stupid idea this was, Danny thought. *To come out here and try to spend a few days living in a tent, climbing a mountain even though I have no experience climbing, and doing it all by myself without another soul in sight!*

If he were able to retrace his steps back to the car then he could head home and hopefully arrive before midnight. Suddenly, off in the distance, he saw some smoke rising, a very welcoming sign. Somebody else was obviously out here being as foolish as he was, so he headed in their direction.

Sure enough, as he approached the fire, there on a log sat an old, tall, slender, bearded fellow with tattered clothing. The man looked up and met Danny's eyes. He seemed completely un-phased to find another person randomly wandering in the woods. Then, as if he had known Danny his whole life, he calmly said, "Hello, friend."

"Umm . . . hi," Danny awkwardly replied. "I'm kind of lost and looking to find my car, which should be right at the foot of the mountain. Any idea where I can pick up a trail to get to the bottom?"

Danny awaited directions, but the old man decided to greet Danny instead. "It's great to meet you. My name is James."

"It's nice to meet you as well. I'm Danny and I'm kind of in a rush, so if you don't mind just letting me know the way . . . ."

"The way to where?"

"The way to my car."

"Why do you want to go to your car?"

"So I can go home."

"Why are you here?"

"I came to climb the mountain."

"Did you climb it?"

"Yes . . . well, no, not really. I tried, but it was a stupid idea, so I'm heading back."

"Why did you want to climb the mountain?"

"Does it matter? Can't you just tell me where to go?"

"Why did you want to climb the mountain?"

"To get to the top! Why else would someone climb a mountain?"

"So you are quitting?"

"No—I mean, yes, I'm quitting. I should have taken my wife's advice and just sat on a beach and relaxed for a few days and played some golf."

James smiled and said, "Okay. I will help you, just follow me."

James led Danny around the brush, over a creek, and down a very steep incline. Danny realized he would never have found his way back on his own. James knew the way so well it was as if he had paved it himself. He looked old and very feeble but was far from it. James effortlessly glided down the mountain, while Danny stumbled around like a blind drunk.

As they reached Danny's car, James looked him in the eyes and said, "I can help you."

"With what?"

"I can help you get started on your journey. I'll be your guide. The mountain can be terrifying with its steep, rocky inclines, loose ground, and the occasional starving bear. Also, there is some very bad weather in store for us over the next few days, but I'll climb with you if you want to take this journey."

"Okay. Is that your best sale? As great as all that sounds, my wife sent me here for a vacation. Anywhere close by where I can find a beach and a tiki bar?"

"That's not exactly my area of expertise. It sounds like you're looking for something I cannot offer you. But it was a pleasure walking with you." And with that, James turned to walk away.

Danny realized how embarrassing it would be to tell his friends and wife he had quit even before he began. Here was a guy offering to guide him, and he seemed to know his way around the place. "Hey—wait up!" Danny shouted. "I'm in. Let's do it."

"Are you sure?"

"Yes—I'm not one to run from a challenge. I wanted to do this on my own, but I can tell that would be foolish. I would like for you to be my guide."

"Great! I'm excited to work with you, Danny. Climbing this mountain is much like life! Lots of ups, some downs, and plenty of obstacles along the way. But we will power through them and surrender to whatever outcome we might find. I will keep an eye on you, and you keep an eye on me. We need the support of one another to reach our destination. No one man can do it alone. In life, we need a few people to care for us along the way; you know, people that will walk by our side and sometimes lead when you feel lost. There is nothing better than a friend or mentor who cares for us and looks out for our best interest. Do you have anybody like that in your life?"

Danny thought for a moment. "Well, I guess my wife, Brownie. She has always guided me along the way and offered insight and love."

"Great! I'm sure you're incredibly grateful for her support. Now, it's important for you to make camp every night in a good location to ensure you will be safe from the elements in case of bad weather. For tonight, a great spot lays just within those trees."

"Wait, *every* night? Can't we just do this today? Surely with your skill and knowledge, we can be up and back before nightfall. I want to climb this mountain and get home."

James laughed. "The man on top of the mountain didn't fall there, Danny. You have a great deal to learn. Our climb will take days at this time of year, since we're working with a limited amount of sunlight. And with many conditions outside of our control, we can never be fully sure we will make it. Still, we will take it one step at a time."

"Whoa, whoa, whoa. Hold up." Danny dramatically put his hands in the air. "Days? And we may not even make it there? What type of guide are you? I'm not sure I want to do this."

"And that is okay! But know this if you do decide to set out on this journey: it will be a transformational experience. I have taken it hundreds of times, and I'm further transformed by every single trek."

Transformational, Danny thought. *Again, with that word.* Danny paused again. He was unsure if he should stay or go, but something inside of him kept buzzing in his ears about how he'd feel if he simply abandoned the journey before he even took the first steps. His pride got the best of him, and he looked at James with a half-hearted sense of confidence.

"Okay, I'm in. Set up camp and then do what?"

James reached inside his bag and pulled out a leather-bound journal and two books. The titles of the books were *The Complete Idiot's Guide to Hiking* and *InSideOut Coaching*. "These are some of the most critical tools for your journey." He handed them to Danny, who looked at them, dumbfounded.

"What are these? No fancy climbing shoes or gear? No map of the mountain? A blank notebook, a book for idiots, and a book on coaching. Really? This has got to be some kind of joke."

"You coach basketball, right?"

"You can tell?"

"It says so on your shirt. 'Washington Prep Basketball.'" James chuckled. Danny even chuckled. "Yes, well . . . at least, for now I do."

"Great! You'll enjoy these books. And since we don't have television or Internet out here, your options are limited! Books are a fantastic way to surround ourselves with some of the brightest people in the history of the world! Not only can they educate us, but they can lift us up, even when everyone else around us is trying to tear us down. The authors of great books and the stories of amazing people can be the most meaningful mentors in our lives."

"I do like to read, but I never have enough time for it. I have a whole bookshelf at home of books I have never read."

"John Waters, the famous author and filmmaker, once said, 'Nothing is more important than an unread library.' I'm sure you'd agree that we make time for what we value! The great news is, you will have less distractions out here to keep you from what is really important. There will be plenty of time for you to not only read these books, but really think about their meaning."

"Okay, I get your point, but what about the blank notebook? Let me guess; you want me to write my deepest, darkest secrets in here, right? Dear Diary . . . blah, blah, blah."

"Danny—every person has a story. Part of your time out here is to discover *your* story, understand it, and interpret the experiences along the way that have shaped you. Great leaders must first know themselves!"

"That sounds really deep and serious. I'm trying to get away from all that on my trip here and just climb to the top of this mountain."

"Whether you realize it or not, I sense you are here for something greater than reaching the top of the mountain. If you want to be a better coach, husband, and father, then you first have to become a better you. Start small. Today, just commit to reading each book for just two minutes. Then take two minutes and write in that blank journal. Seems simple enough, doesn't it?"

"What should I write about?"

"Start by writing down the many things you're grateful for in your life."

"Okay, I can do that."

"Great, I'll see you tomorrow morning. We move at daylight."

And at that, he was gone. Danny spent the next hour setting up his tent and making a small fire to keep himself warm. He had planned on cooking some meat and eating some healthy vegetables that his wife packed for him, but Danny ended up snacking on potato chips instead.

> **Reflect and write: Take a few minutes to write down all the things in your life for which you are grateful.**

Still, he got out his journal and started writing down all the things he was grateful for in his life. He thought it to be such a simple exercise, but he struggled along the way. He had so many wonderful things in his life, yet he realized how little he focused on them. As he did this, he started to come to terms with just how insufferable he had been these last few months, constantly complaining and grumpy with the people who loved him the most. He didn't even like being around himself! But at the end of the journaling, he felt a sense of gratitude and clarity around all that was good in his life. He decided he would have his players do this as well when they started their training camp.

He started reading after journaling. *InSideOut Coaching*, he thought. *Sounds boring.* But then two minutes turned into ten minutes. And ten into an hour. And an hour into four hours, which was the exact time it took Danny to finish the book.

Funny enough, Danny realized that James had baited him into the reading and journaling process. James knew Danny would agree to a couple of minutes just to shut him up. But Danny quickly got hooked and thoroughly enjoyed the book. That motivated him to dive a little deeper and start writing down his own reflections. While the day started off with some challenges, Danny felt quite satisfied with the small yet impactful steps he had taken.

With no lights or distractions in sight, as it grew dark, Danny nodded off to sleep.

CHAPTER 4

CREATE A MISSION

Bitter cold and wind welcomed Danny's second day of his journey. Since it was still winter, and the sunlight was scarce, Danny and his newly "hired" guide didn't want to delay their start. So they were on their way after eating some breakfast and packing up their gear. James had explained it would be a long day of hiking, and they had better be prepared to make camp. The terrain seemed quite easy as they set out, and both were quiet along the way. They enjoyed listening and taking in the beautiful morning sounds.

But things started to get more difficult after a while. Some of the areas were steep, but others were just completely overrun with brush. There was no trail as far as Danny could see. It became very clear to Danny that few people had tried to hike up this mountain. It wasn't the tallest in the area, but it had a reputation for being irritably difficult. He was beginning to understand exactly why!

Danny was out of breath and needed a break from climbing and practically crawling through some of the brush-covered areas. As he stopped to drink some water, James asked him the first of many questions. "Why do you want to hike this mountain?"

"Not this again! I told you. So I can get to the top."

"Why do you want to get to the top?"

"Well . . . I heard there is a great view up there."

"Why not find a taller mountain nearby with a better view? There are plenty of mountains with great views that you can easily drive up these days."

"True. Maybe I should have done that." Danny smiled. "I guess I wanted to do something challenging. Get outdoors and away from people."

"So, you are hiking for the experience?"

"Yes, I guess you're correct. I thought it would be a fun experience, and while some parts are already incredibly challenging, I'm enjoying it so far. Also, you said each hike up this mountain helped to transform you. I want that experience. I think I *need* that experience, even though I'm not exactly sure what that might feel like."

"You're very astute! We never fully know what experiences life will give us, and it's the unexpected experiences and challenges that provide the opportunity for the greatest personal transformation. So, if you're hiking up this mountain just for the experience of doing so, does it even really matter if you reach the top or not?"

"Of course it does! Who sets out hiking up a mountain with no goal to reach the top? I need to be able to go home and say, 'I did it!'"

James paused for a moment. "So is the hike your mission or the goal?"

Danny hadn't thought about it that way. "Well, my goal is to get to the top. That's why I keep going. My mission? Well isn't that the same thing? To get to the top?"

"What if you try to achieve your goal and fail? What if you fall and break your leg? What if a blizzard hits and your chances of survival drop? Are you going to push through that and risk abandoning your family? What if you found another traveler wounded in the forest and he needed immediate help? Would you abandon your hike to save his life?"

"Well, I guess I would have a good excuse for not achieving my goal!"

"Exactly! An excuse. We can come up with excuses and even some valid reasons for not achieving a goal. We can evade or brush off responsibility for a whole host of different reasons. What would happen, Danny, if instead of setting the goal of hiking up the mountain, you just had a mission?"

"A *mission*—a bartender back home told me I needed one of those." Danny thought back to his conversation with Auggie.

"Why are you hiking up this mountain?"

"To grow stronger."

"Why don't you just use a stair climber at the gym? That will help you develop muscle as well, you know."

Danny laughed. "No, I want to grow stronger *as a person*. I need to discover some things about myself by being challenged, being silent, and listening."

"I really like your thinking. Use the experience; don't let the experience use you. Now, use your 'why' to craft your mission for the next few days. The difference between your mission and your goal is that your goal is your desired outcome or result, like getting to the top of the mountain. Your goals can also be smaller steps, like hiking ten miles each day. But your mission is a much deeper calling. It's your purpose. For example, the goal of your basketball team is to win the championship, but your mission is to build a team that plays well together, supports one another, and works hard on a daily basis to grow and develop as a unit. If you live your projected mission, you will inch closer to achieving your goal."

Danny thought for a while. "I'm hiking up this mountain to grow in self-knowledge and mental strength. I suppose that's my mission."

"I like it. An invaluable experience is on the horizon. Regardless of the circumstances, you can live that every second of this climb. You have a mission, and you are working to fulfill it with each small step. Tonight, once we set up camp, take a few minutes and actually write down your mission. That is something we should all do for every specific goal we set. Try it. I think it will help guide you moving forward."

As they started to walk again, Danny quietly considered the conversation they just had. James broke the silence by telling him a story.

"Centuries ago, villages in Ireland took great pride in building beautiful churches. One village saved money for decades, so they could build the most magnificent church for their community. When they had the money together, they formed a committee to interview three different stonemasons for the job. They visited three stonemasons, who all were working on other churches for neighboring villages. During the interview, they asked each one a very simple question: 'What are you doing?' The first said, 'I'm cutting, preparing, and building with stones.' The second said, 'I'm building a church.' The third said, 'I'm building the house of God.' Get it? The first stonemason sees it as a job. The second sees it as a career. The third sees it as a calling. Who do you think the village chose? Danny, how do you view coaching? Job, career, or calling? Are you coaching a sport, building a team, or are you building young men?"

Danny thought for a bit, mulling the question over. "I've never really thought of it that way. I guess I just always saw myself as a coach. The more I think about it, the more I realize I want something more. Reading that book last night really got me thinking. I don't want to be just a coach or even a teacher of the game. I want my players to view me as a mentor."

James nodded in agreement. "Our world doesn't need more basketball coaches; our world needs more mentors and educators in sports. We need leaders, those special people that shape lives, not jumpers."

"I didn't start coaching with the idea of winning in my head. I just wanted to help kids have fun and get better. But something changed along the way. I think I would tell myself that I was coaching to make a difference, but after a while, my identity got so caught up in being a 'basketball coach' that I needed to win games to validate myself as a person. I keep noticing failed relationships in my life, because I think young people—and even adults—can sense that in me."

Danny grew incredibly sad as it became very clear to him that he had lost his way and missed an opportunity to make a difference in the lives of his players. Some of them were now running the streets. He thought about a former player named Troy, and how he had recently gotten locked up for armed robbery.

If he hadn't been so concerned about winning all the time, he could have used sports to pass on positive life messages and build character. If he hadn't been so concerned about what the players could do for him, he could have done more for the players.

James looked into his eyes. Sensing his pain, he said, "We do the best we can with what we know. You have an incredible heart, Danny, but don't forget that as a coach, you have incredible power, and thus, responsibility. The irony is that when you prioritize character over winning, you typically end up winning more. This is because better people make better athletes. So, what is your mission in coaching?"

"Well, I really like the one I read in the book last night!" Danny pulled out his journal and read the quote he had written down: "To help boys become men of empathy and integrity who will lead, be responsible, and change the world for good."[3]

"Awesome. Nobody and nothing except you can stop you from living your mission. A mission doesn't just give you direction, it gives you drive. Research shows that the more connected you are to your purpose, the grittier you are!"

"Grittier?"

"We'll discuss more of that later. Before we get going, let me give you this book. It's called *Wooden on Leadership*, and it's by the greatest coach of all time."

"*Another book?*"

"Yep, but for now, let's get moving!"

Reflect and write: Why do you coach?

The journey became more and more challenging over the next few miles. Not just due to the mountain, but because Danny was overweight and not conditioned for this type of activity. He had eaten only junk food in the last sixteen hours. On top of that, his feet ached, and he had blisters. Danny tried as hard as he could to push through the exhaustion, but he felt off-balance and dizzy. He could only think of how tired and hungry he was.

---

3   *InSideOut Coaching: How Sports Can Transform Lives* by Joe Ehrmann

Distracted, he slipped on a rock, falling flat on his face against the side of the mountain. In doing so, he violently banged his knee. Pain shot through his entire leg, and he rolled over, moaning and clutching his knee.

CHAPTER 5

DEFINE CORE VALUES

James helped Danny sit down to tend to his knee. He could see that Danny was dizzy. Danny's knee was badly bruised and numbed by pain. Walking would be hard enough, but hiking in these conditions with only a few hours of daylight left seemed impossible. They would have to make camp here. Without judgment, James asked, "What can you learn from this experience?"

"Be more careful, I guess? I don't know, sometimes we just fall, and we've got to keep moving forward."

James laughed. "Danny, that sounds good and might make a great line in a *Rocky* movie, but every setback or challenge provides you with an opportunity to learn and grow. So, what can you learn from this experience?"

"Well . . . I was getting dizzy. I haven't eaten much, and what I have eaten has been mostly junk food. I'm definitely out of shape and overweight. On top of that, my feet are starting to get sores from all this walking."

"Good assessment. Sometimes, we will fail because we lack experience, but other times, we fail because we don't prepare. Did you read the hiking book I gave you?"

"No, it was too boring!"

"Sometimes we have to read boring things to learn important things! If you had read the first chapter, it would have reminded you to warm up, stretch, eat nutritious food, stay focused, and even correctly put on your socks. Any chance you might think those would be helpful lessons right now?"

Danny sighed, allowing James's sarcasm to fully set in. "Okay, okay, I get you. I have always been pretty good at learning lessons the hard way, and this is no different. I'll be sure to read some more of the hiking book today and do the little things, so I'm ready tomorrow. It's not like I can do much else at this point. If I have my energy back tomorrow and my knee under me, do you think we can reach the summit?"

"No offense, Danny, but you lack technical experience, conditioning, and you're significantly overweight, so we will have to take it slow and keep it simple. You fall like that again, and a helicopter will be the only way you make it off this mountain. Don't make the mistake of thinking you can avoid the struggles and failures of this experience. That's where you will gain the strength and experience to climb the mountain." After a pause, he continued, "Coaching is the same way, Danny! Many people look for a quick fix. They think they can build their program's culture and the character of their team by hiring a motivational speaker, paying for a leadership course, or taking their team on a three-day retreat in the mountains. Yes, they can help. So can an energy bar and a good night's rest. But the sports field presents challenges and resistance that can be used to cultivate virtue and strength of character, almost like how we build up muscle. We need to repeatedly put ourselves under stress, even to the point of failure at times."

Danny nodded in understanding. "The coaching book you gave me, *InSideOut Coaching*, mentioned the very idea of training character and said that I have to decide what my core values are. It reminded me that deciding what is important is very important!"

"Exactly. Now let's set up camp, so you can eat and rest. Start thinking about the greatest coach you ever had and the qualities you admired about them the most!"

James and Danny set up their camp, ate a hearty lunch, and then James headed off on a walk. Meanwhile, Danny sat and read his latest book on John Wooden. He found himself lost in the content, reading for hours. The book was rich and full of ideas to build a transformational culture, and Danny scribbled rapidly in his notebook.

Years ago, he had passed out John Wooden's *Pyramid of Success* to his teams. This pyramid taught fifteen different values in a hierarchy of importance that outlined a process for building character. Danny still loved it, and it seemed so comprehensive, but he knew he would need to start by simply choosing the most core values necessary and creating his own language that he and his players could relate to. Danny remembered reading this book, and he would never forget the core values it outlined. Just like he had taken notes on the *Pyramid of Success*, Danny started to do the same for this recent Wooden addition to his hiking library. When he was done, he looked over his notes on John Wooden's core values, and every one of them seemed absolutely critical! Still, he knew it was important to start small and be faithful to just one of them, if that's what it would take. It was then that he thought about James's question: *What are the qualities I admired most in the greatest coach I have known?*

Reflect and write: Who is the greatest coach you have ever known? What qualities did you admire most about them?

As Danny finished writing his core values, James returned with some fish he caught, sat down by the fire with Danny, and prepared the fish for cooking. *This guy can do everything*, Danny thought to himself. *Hike, fish, and offer life lessons in the process.* As Danny's thoughts wondered in the direction of James's remarkable survival skills, James spoke up: "Well, how is it coming?"

"Pretty good. I was thinking a lot about my old coach from eighth grade, his name was Coach Watson. I wrote down three qualities that I admired about him the most. He loved us, he worked hard, and he never gave up on me, no matter how many times I screwed up. That's the coach I want to be." Danny then shared what he believed were his three most comprehensive core values and how he defined each of these values:

1. **Love Others.** Eagerly and selflessly serve others, not yourself.
2. **Work Deeply.** Build habits of joyfully giving your best physically, intellectually, emotionally, and mentally.
3. **Be Resilient.** Overcome fear, doubt, and failure to do the best you can within your circumstances.

James was impressed by the simplicity and depth of Danny's core values. "Developing your core values is something that will be a never-ending process," James said. "Even the great John Wooden constantly revised his pyramid of success late in life. The challenge now is to bring these to life, in your own life and the lives of the people you lead! While it's important and motivating to write out your core values, many teams and organizations already have these, just like they have a mission. The real challenge is to actualize these core values. When you actualize a core value, it becomes a virtue or a character strength."

Danny knew this to be true. "Every season, I sit down and write out my vision for the season, but when it comes to turning the vision into action, I seem to fail miserably. How do I make it happen?"

"It doesn't start with motivational talks, character curriculums, or fancy slogans. Danny, what does John Wooden say it starts with?"

Danny looked in his notebook and read the poem:[4]

"No written word

No spoken plea

Can teach our youth what they should be

Nor all the books

On all the shelves.

---

4   Attributed to Rudyard Kipling

It's what the teachers are themselves."

James smiled. "Exactly. The most powerful leadership tool is *you*. The team will become a reflection of their coach. Start by looking in the mirror and seeing how you reflect your core values."

A light seemed to turn on in Danny's head. "That's why I need the transformation of being! I've been serving myself instead of others for a while now, so how could I expect that of my players?"

"Yes! Only after you start to be the example can you focus on the next step in the process. Then you can start shaping your strategies, procedures, and behaviors around your core values. Now get some rest; we have the opportunity to do some challenging climbs tomorrow!"

CHAPTER 6

DEVELOP A GROWTH MINDSET

Even with a throbbing knee, Danny was so exhausted he had a great night's sleep. He awoke to the first few rays of sunlight beaming down on his face, warming him in the process. Danny and James started by eating a good, high-protein breakfast of bird eggs James had scavenged from trees, and then quickly packed up camp. Everyday James did something that just blew Danny's mind. Before they began their third day of hiking, Danny double checked his gear and ensured he had correctly put on his socks.

Last night, Danny realized there were blisters on the sides of his feet because he had carelessly put his socks on, leaving wrinkles and bunching in his hiking shoes. *Rookie mistake*, he thought. The irony was that he had only read the day before how the legendary coach John Wooden spent the first fifteen minutes of every season teaching his All-American basketball players how to put on their socks. Danny was starting to realize that the little things make a huge difference.

As they hiked, Danny and James came to a side of the mountain that looked more like a cliff than an incline. James suggested that Danny should follow behind him, so he could walk him through each step. But stubborn as he was, Danny brushed him off. Just like so many others, he was out to prove his strength to the old man. Danny started up, using small trees and rocks to pull himself up the steepest parts of the incline. The more he climbed, the more nervous and unsure of himself he became. It had looked much simpler from below. Suddenly, Danny couldn't see where he could possibly go next. He was stuck. There was nothing to grab onto in sight, and so he started to panic.

James called up to him from twenty feet below, as if his distress was glaring. "Need any help?"

Danny, unwilling to accept he was stuck, ignored the offer and instead tried to move sideways around the rock that jutted out in front of him. Worry crept over him, and he knew James could sense his fear. He side-stepped along the slope, and his foot met an insecure rock, causing him to lose his footing. Luckily, some small tree limbs were in his way along the twenty-foot drop, and they broke his fall as he landed right on his back.

James hurried over to Danny, who was sprawled out on the ground, wincing in pain and barely able to breath. "Are you okay?"

Danny struggled to respond, but between gasping breaths, he said, "I'm fine! We shouldn't be climbing this part of the mountain anyway. Surely there's a safer part to climb. I'm not sure why you chose this one. It almost feels like you're trying to kill me out here."

"Sometimes, the harder path is what's best for us. Why did you insist on going ahead? I asked you to let me lead."

"Well, I trusted you when you said that this was the best way. I didn't think it would be some impossible deathtrap! I wanted to prove to you that I was strong and capable. You're over forty years older than me and shouldn't be the one leading this climb. I can handle this—or at least I thought I could."

"The mountain is not a test, and this journey is not a test. We're on a journey, and if you continue to see it as a test, you will continue to miss out on the most valuable part: the opportunity to learn and grow. Stop trying to prove yourself to me or pass the test. Why don't you try to see what you might actually learn from this experience? Did that fall of yours offer you any immediate lessons?"

"Hell yeah, it did. I learned that I couldn't climb this part of the mountain!"

"If you think you can't, then you're right. If you think you can, then you're right. Sometimes our greatest challenges are actually our greatest opportunities. Randy Pausch, a professor at Carnegie Melon, once said, 'Brick walls are there for a reason; they give us a chance to see how badly we want something.' So, how badly do you want it? You're facing an incredible challenge. You will fall, and it will hurt. But if something is worth doing, then it is worth doing wrong and failing until you can do it right!"

"Yeah? I get all that. But I seriously doubt that Randy thinks risking your life to climb a mountain is a good idea. You aren't going to accomplish much if your life is over."

"Well the truth is that some things *are* worth risking your life over. In life, everyone should ask themselves a pretty important question: What am I willing to die for? It would be pretty simple if this experience was just about getting to the top to prove people wrong. But if this journey is about personal growth and becoming the person the world needs you to be, then getting to the top isn't even the goal in the first place."

"What? It is totally irrational to suggest I do a bunch of things I'm going to fail at. Why would anyone actively search out failure? It just sounds like you'd be looking for trouble in that sense."

"Because our greatest opportunities to grow aren't found by coasting through a life of meaningless achievements. Anyone can do that. We evolve by addressing the failures we experience when we live a meaningful life, and by taking on some of our greatest challenges in pursuit of something greater than ourselves! Sometimes you have to stretch yourself to the limit of failure to see exactly what you're made of."

Danny thought about the decision he was facing with coaching. "This conversation really makes me wonder whether I should return to coaching the Washington Prep Warriors. Right now, I'm paralyzed by the fear of knowing that it won't just be hard, but I will probably fail. And the worst part is that failure will really hurt. The administration will probably dress me down, and they'll almost surely fire me if I don't exceed expectations this next season."

"You can escape life's challenges for only so long." James looked up at the side of the mountain. "But someday life—just like this mountain—will throw unavoidable challenges your way. You will need the strength that the hard path has built within you. And when you fall on your back, you will have only one choice—to get up and keep climbing."

"What about my family? What if nobody wants to hire me after I get fired? I need to support my wife and children. Sometimes, the risks affect more than just yourself."

"And if the worst-case scenario happens—if you lose your job and your house, and you and your family are out on the street—they will at least have a husband and father who has faced his fears, lived by his principles, and used everything to shape himself into a better man. And you will use whatever setback or challenge that comes next as an opportunity to learn and grow as a family!"

Danny pondered this reality. "Wow—that sure does calm my nerves. We will live in a box and beg for money, but at least my family will respect me. I just fell twenty feet onto my back on some really hard rocks. I literally hit rock bottom. And now you're encouraging me to possibly head toward rock bottom in my coaching career? This fall hurt enough. I'm not sure I'm interested in experiencing it again."

"'Rock bottom became the solid foundation on which I rebuilt my life.' Danny, do you know who said that? An abused, divorced, single mother on welfare, who was also a jobless, depressed, unpublished writer. Sounds like she had a lot going for her, right? She wrote a manuscript called *Harry Potter and the Philosopher's Stone*. I hope you don't have to experience rock bottom like J. K. Rowling did, but you have little control over what happens to you in life. It's the ten-ninety rule. Life is ten percent what happens to you and ninety percent how you react to it. We all have a story—we can let our failures become that story, or we can choose persistence and courage to do what we need to do when what we need to do is most difficult. Those are the stories that stay with you. Had J. K. simply given up on her dream, the world would have never known the little boy with glasses and a lightning bolt scar on his head. Those are some of my favorite books to read under the stars."

Danny always believed he was meant for something special. The problem was that he had started listening to the world when it told him he wasn't worthy. But now he was beginning to believe in himself again, just by listening to James. "I remember how Steve Jobs and Apple failed at making a CD-R player back in the day, but due to that failure, they came up with the most innovative MP3 player on the market. Without that failure, they would never have gone on to create things like the iPhone. I really have to move past my fear of failure."

Danny started to climb again, but this time James was close behind, encouraging him. As he faced the challenging terrain, James helped him to find the safe path and overcome the challenging hike one step at a time. Danny felt encouraged after reaching the top without another fall. He continued on, with a new energy and conviction that regardless of the challenges, he was going to learn and grow from the experience. In that moment, Danny had switched from a fixed mindset where he wouldn't develop, to a growth-oriented mindset where he could start to face the challenges in his path and overcome them.

After a few more challenging climbs, Danny turned to James. "I'm starting to enjoy these challenging climbs! Every time I start to get afraid, I move past that fear and look for an opportunity to grow. The more I overcome that fear, the more I realize it's not that bad. It's like going to the doctor—much worse in your mind than in reality."

"You're developing a growth mindset!"

"A what?"

"It's called a growth mindset. Carol Dweck, a researcher out of Stanford University, did some groundbreaking performance psychology research on the difference between really talented, successful people and those who don't make it. She found that those who made it had a growth mindset, and the others had a fixed mindset."

"What's the difference?"

"People with a growth mindset don't just *seek* challenges, they *thrive* on challenges." James went on to explain the key differences then gave him the book *Mindset* by Carol Dweck for his reading that evening.

"I'm over eighty years old, and I have gone through a lot in my lifetime. If I could do things differently, I would have spent more time with the people I loved, read more books, and taken on greater challenges. However, I would *not* try to bypass my failures or the painful moments, because I'm sure those have shaped me. Don't forget your greatest challenges are your greatest opportunities!"

> **Reflect and write: What are some of your biggest failures? How did they provide an opportunity to learn and grow? What is the worst-case scenario you face in coaching? How might that be a foundation on which to build from?**

Danny realized that deciding not to return for another year of coaching would be a fear-based decision. He didn't want to keep living in fear anymore.

All of a sudden, dark clouds loomed overhead. James looked up and said, "Looks like a big storm is coming. We're going to have to set up camp and wait this one out."

CHAPTER 7
MAKE COMMITMENTS

As Danny drifted in and out of sleep, he could hear the soft pitter-patter of rain falling onto his tent. He also saw flashes of light in the sky, which completely lit up the otherwise dark mountain. While it was somewhat concerning, considering they were sitting ducks in the middle of the forest, it was a magnificent sight to see, reminding Danny of the mystery and power of nature. The tapping of the rain on his tent was therapeutic, and he eventually fell into a deep sleep.

When Danny woke up the next morning—the fourth day of his journey—it was still downpouring. He focused his eyes on the top of his tent, and watched the raindrops bounce off. This went on for hours, and at times it seemed like the downpour would never subside. It was only hours later that the rain slowed, and Danny was finally able to get up and out of his tent.

Danny found James journaling quietly in his tent. "Hey, James, the rain isn't that bad, don't you think we can get going?"

"We're very close to the summit, but this is by far the most dangerous part of our journey. Even the most experienced climber of Clearview Mountain knows that it would be a bad choice to take on that challenge right now. The rain will make it difficult and slippery, and we have already seen how you deal with slippery inclines."

"What about seeking our greatest challenges?! I'm ready for it!"

James laughed. "I appreciate your enthusiasm! But sometimes, the greatest challenge is to be disciplined, patient, and wait for the right moment. We have a lot to gain today from our time in the rain."

"What do we have to gain from sitting around here in our tents and doing nothing? I only have seven days to reach my goal, and we're on the fourth day going nowhere! That's not going to help me at all."

"Remember, that's one of the many great dangers of setting goals; it can lead us into making unwise decisions and going against our principles, or what we know in our hearts to be the right decision. Should you hike that last leg and find you cannot navigate the difficult terrain, you'll lose more than just a great opportunity. "

"I know, I know. I even read it in Carol Dweck's book last night. She discusses her research, which showed that setting performance goals—like an A plus on a test—hurt the students' learning. Instead, people should set *learning* goals—task-oriented goals to improve mastery and competence. I mean, I get what she is saying, and it makes sense in a vacuum. But as a guy with goals and desires, it is really hard not to focus on achieving them. I'm not really sure how I can just push the off button on that and set learning goals. I suppose I can try, but I just think focusing on my goals will creep in and block out everything else."

"You have to work hard to fall in love with the process, and when you do, the process will love you back! That is a growth mindset. In our culture, it's not easy to break free from this mindset, because everyone is expected to set goals. If you don't have some big goal of reaching the peak, winning the championship, or becoming a big-time division one college coach, then people would almost surely think: he must not be a competitor, or he must not want it that badly. People judge others by their goals, when what we *should* care about is what they are committed to doing."

"I can understand that. But we aren't always the one setting our goals. What if other people set goals for us? My principal does a pretty good job of telling me what success looks like in our season. He sets the goals, and if I don't achieve them, then it really doesn't matter if the process was a good one or not. For him, the end justifies the means. So it's not as simple for me."

James replied, "Does worrying and focusing on the goal help? No. What you need to be focused on is your commitments. Some people call them 'controllable goals', 'learning goals', or 'actionable goals'. If you still want to hold onto having goals, then call them that. Or just let your principal label them as one of those terms. It doesn't matter much what you call them; what matters is what you're willing to do, not what you say you are going to do."

"You can't build a reputation on what you are going to do!" Danny exclaimed. "We stuck that up in our locker room this year. I stole it from the University of North Carolina women's soccer team. It's funny; I have been telling my players for years to 'control the controllables', but the whole time, I've been an emotional wreck focused on the scoreboard and whether we are going to win a championship. I didn't really care about anything else, and certainly didn't spend a lot of time focusing on the process."

"Exactly! People like goals, because they bring structure and order to their vision of the future. It's like a target for an archer; something that is real and tangible. The problem is that you aren't organizing the present— the here and now. You sacrifice the process for the goal. You can't enjoy the process when you're focused on the future, because the only way to experience joy is by attaining your goal. It is a dangerous cycle for most. However, the craziest part of it all is that when we finally attain that goal, the joy ends up being very short-lived! We just move on to the next one and rarely even celebrate what we just achieved."

Danny grew excited. "I need to start finding happiness in the pursuit, not pursuing happiness!"

James nodded encouragingly. "Don't get distracted by your goals. You need to start shifting your daily habits. A change in your daily habits will lead to the transformation of being that you and everyone else so desperately seeks, whether they realize it or not. A friend of mind would always remind me, 'It isn't about what you want. It's about what you are willing to do to close the gap between who you are and who you want to become.'"[5]

Danny replied, "You know, now that you mention it, I remember hearing Brad Stevens, the coach of the Boston Celtics, saying, 'I know it sounds strange, but I don't really have goals. I focus on getting better every single day.' John Wooden didn't care about goals, either; he was always saying that he was too focused on the process. His players say they never heard him talk about winning. So how do I get there? I have been listening and trying to emulate these coaches for years, and I'm still too caught up in my goals, even when they tell me not to be. On those rare occasions when we wouldn't talk about winning in the locker room, I would still be thinking: I need to win this game! So it was a complete farce. A total joke. I tried to make my players believe in this approach when I couldn't even buy in."

"Well, what would your day look like if you were a hundred percent committed to becoming the best coach you could be? What if you simply forgot about winning or losing and just put your head down and worked hard? Would it be anything like it is now?"

Danny thought for a while. *How do I spend my time?* The more he thought, the more he realized his energy was wasted on what he couldn't control, "unwinding" after a long day by watching mindless TV shows and reading and commenting on social media feeds instead of reading books and journaling. Just in the last few days, he had gotten so much from the few hours he had spent reading and reflecting.

"I guess I waste most of my day, really," Danny said, feeling kind of embarrassed. "Time is the one resource that we can't buy more of, and how I choose to spend my time says a lot about what I value. Pretty embarrassing, when I think about it. I have always known just how valuable of a resource time can be, yet I didn't care for it or treat it with respect. I clearly piss away way too much time."

---

5   *The Principle Circle* by Jamie Gilbert

....

Reflect and write: Close the gap between who you are and who you want to be with two commitments. What is one thing you can start doing and one thing you can stop doing to close the gap? Start today!

....

"Well, part of it is focusing on your relationship with time. The reason why time slips away is because we forget just how important it can be. Let's try something just to make you a little more aware about time. First, envision the best day ever; one in which you challenge and stretch yourself. Write all that in your journal. Then start small, even with something that will only take two to five minutes. What is the one thing you can start doing tomorrow? What is the one thing you can *stop* doing tomorrow? The truth is that we need to intentionally decide what *not* to do, if we're going to make time for the things we *need* to do. It sounds silly, but your first commitment could be to sit down and decide what you are committed to doing that day! We have to start somewhere. Every day, add more time to a certain commitment or make a new commitment. Try to add these things on top of something you already do and build it into a routine. The interesting thing about time is that as you start to focus on it, you seem to have more of it at your disposal. Now, we all only have twenty-four hours in each day, but how we use those twenty-four hours is what separates success from failure."

Danny felt motivated. James didn't tell him what he had to do; he just encouraged him to start taking small steps toward building a better process. Danny had plenty to think about for the rest of the rainy day.

Still, he couldn't help but think he was running out of time if he wanted to reach the summit.

CHAPTER 8
PRINCIPLES TO GUIDE US

It was the fifth day of their journey together, and while it had taken Danny difficult lesson after lesson, he finally bought into the direction and guidance James had continuously tried to offer him. It was probably a good thing, since Danny was unsure of just how many more falls his now frail body could take. He had been hardheaded and unwilling to listen at first, but the mountain had quickly offered him awareness. It wasn't graceful and it wasn't gentle, but sometimes the most effective lessons are those we learn the hard way.

While Danny had found a growing level of confidence in his ability to hike the steep incline, he still knew James's experience would keep them both on the right path and prevent any careless mistakes. The ground was still a little slick from all the rain, and the high winds had caused many branches to fall on the ground. If this terrain wasn't safe before the storm hit, it was an absolute deathtrap now. Remaining humble and listening to James would be Danny's only chance at a successful climb.

In fact, this might have been one of the greatest lessons Danny learned to this point. He needed help in life. Moving forward, perhaps Danny could do a better job of leaning on those people around him who were willing to assist him through difficult times. No man is an island, Danny remembered, and he felt determined to remind himself of that once he arrived home from this journey.

During their hike, Danny would often come to a point where it seemed he could go in multiple directions. He also knew each decision would bring its own set of outcomes, some which might be good (like easy passage), and others that might bring challenges (like falling on his ass again). It seemed like he had to ask James every few minutes: "Which way?" Finally, tired of having to continuously ask where to go next, he turned to James and asked, "How do you know where we are supposed to go next? In those first few miles of our climb there were markers of where people had walked before, but as we have gotten higher, I'm not really seeing anything that leads me in one direction or another. I feel ass-backward here, and I just don't know where to go. And now, with all the rain and wind from yesterday, there are branches everywhere, and they washed away any of the remaining footprints."

"That's a good question!" James exclaimed. "It's important to be strong enough to climb the mountain, but you also have to know which way to go. One without the other will almost inevitably lead you to a literal or metaphorical dead end. Since we are without clear signs of the journey ahead, I have to make my decisions based on principles I carry with me. For example, the 'easy way' is not always the right way. The path most worn is not always the right path. And often, it's not even about choosing the right path, but about traveling the path in the right way. Even the safest route can offer you considerable obstacles if you aren't prepared for them. When I come to a point where I must decide where to go, I just remember my principles and apply them."

"So, you don't just work from experience on the mountain or a feel for the easier terrain?"

"Nope! The mountain is always changing, and experience can only take us so far. If I made decisions based on just my feelings, I would likely allow my emotions to determine my choices, which is a recipe for disaster. Danny, climbing this mountain is just like coaching and life. The choices we make and the actions we take based on how we feel lead to selfishness, broken families, depression, and a very bleak future. Feel alone is not enough. In fact, it can create a devastating outcome—even if we are able to accomplish certain goals in life. However, it is really important to ensure the choices we make and the actions we take are actually in line with our principles. When they are, they often lead to love, joy, and peace—even if we fail to achieve a traditional definition of success. Forget about your feelings. Forget about your situation. The question you really should be working to answer is what principles can you apply in your life that will keep you moving on the right path, growing as a person, and positively influencing the lives of others? Answer that, and you will really be onto something. If you do, you can never lose. You will never fall. You will always succeed."

Danny nodded in understanding. "I think I get it. So if I'm focused on changing my situation, I might miss out on the opportunity to develop my character, which is the mission and purpose of any journey. Instead of making decisions based on emotion, I have to focus on the principles to guide my choices that define who I am and reflect my values. It's starting to make a lot of sense to me."

Reflect and write: What are your principles in life?

"Yes, you're getting ahold of this a lot faster than I did! I was pretty stubborn at your age," James chuckled. "If we approach life with a growth mindset and see everything as an opportunity to learn and improve, then we will continue to develop and apply new principles in life. Let me ask you this: What principles have you learned so far on your journey?"

"I hadn't really thought about that, although I know I have some."

James smiled. "Well, let's try this on for size. We aren't going to hit the summit today, so how about we call it a day just a little early. I say we break for camp, and give you some extra time and a little bit of extra sunlight for you to give your guiding principles some thought. Are you willing to give it a try?"

"Well . . . sure. Why not? I gotta figure this out sometime or another. Might as well be today."

Danny and James then gathered kindling and some larger logs to keep the fire going well into the night. As Danny scoured the nearby area for wood, he started to seriously think about his guiding principles. This wasn't an easy exercise for Danny; not because he didn't have them, but because he had never really thought about them in action. However, what is measured can be improved, and Danny needed clarity in his principles.

After building a fire worthy of the Stone Age, Danny retreated back to his tent while James started on dinner. He grabbed his journal and a pen and started jotting down notes. He then turned his general notes into much more specific and actionable thoughts. By the time James had called him for dinner, Danny threw his journal onto his sleeping bag with the following written down:

Danny's Principles:

1. Everyone wants the opportunity to be a part of something greater than ourselves.
2. The man on top of the mountain didn't fall there.
3. The world doesn't need more coaches; the world needs more mentors.
4. We do the best we can with what we know.
5. Lead with love.

As Danny emerged from his tent he had a look of calmness on his face. He knew he'd be just fine if he could follow these guiding principles. James looked at Danny and said, "So . . . how'd it go? You got something jotted down?" With a sense of pride, Danny answered, "I think I'm onto something here, James. If you can keep us from getting lost tomorrow, then I might just share them with you!"

Without hesitation, James said, "Why don't you show me rather than tell me." Danny shot James a quick smile, thinking to himself how James always seemed to get the last word.

CHAPTER 9

SURRENDER THE DESTINATION

A s the day came to a close, the temperature dropped enough for snow to fall. James and Danny huddled around the roaring fire and wrapped themselves in heavy blankets. The snow was sticking and accumulated quickly. Inch after inch, Danny worried they would once again be delayed. With precious time running out, he would not reach the summit before he had to head home. He had promised Brownie he would be back after a week, and she'd be worried sick if he wasn't timely. They were also running low on basic supplies, like food and toilet paper. He wasn't sure which one concerned him more, but he knew he didn't want to go hungry or use leaves. James broached the topic of holding camp until he felt it safe enough to start climbing again. "No, no, no!" Danny exclaimed. "I'm ready to finish this climb tomorrow, but with the snow, we will never make it now. Even if we *can* climb, it'll be slow moving."

James looked at Danny. "Why are you still so afraid of not reaching the summit?"

Danny paused for a moment, but he couldn't shake the potential of falling short. "I won't get my picture at the top, and everyone is going to see me as a failure! They will just think I packed up all this stuff, drove out to the mountains, and drank beer all week. I will be the laughing stock of the town."

James shook his head. "Even after all your growth and the lessons we've shared, you're still unable to surrender the destination, even though

55

you claim to be all about the journey? A very important truth for you is that if people ever want to close the gap from where they are to where they want to be, they need the faith and courage to surrender the result and accept the possibility that they may not reach their destination. If you're unable to mentally surrender to the fact that you may not reach the summit, then how are you going to have the courage to surrender to the outcome of this season?"

Danny paused for a moment then asked, "If I truly surrender the destination, does that mean I have to give up on my dreams and aspirations of winning a championship, or even just keeping my dream job? Because if that is the case, I'm not sure I'm interested in surrendering anything at all."

"You aren't giving up the fight for your job or the dream of a state championship; you are giving up the belief that you have control over something you don't actually have control over. See the difference between the two? Acknowledging that truth is scary, but acknowledging it and giving your very best with no guarantees is even scarier. When you can push past that fear, it will be one of the most liberating moments of your life."

James looked down and stoked the fire as the snowfall became heavier.

"What if I change and give my very best this season, but the team, the parents, and the administration already have their minds made up about me, and are unwilling to work with me? Frankly, that's one of my greatest fears. And I think that's in part why I just cannot move past this."

James looked up with disappointment in his eyes. "What if? A great question! What if you lose your job, and people fail to give you a second chance? It's a great question to ask! What if you win, and the school has to deal with a budget crisis and fires you anyway? How'd you feel about that? My point is that all you can do is your best and follow your guiding principles. Danny, have you ever heard of Adam Brown?"

"No. Who is he?"

"Adam Brown overcame homelessness and an addiction to crack-cocaine to become a Navy SEAL. After becoming a SEAL, during a mission, he lost vision in his dominant eye and should have been done altogether as a SEAL. Instead, he retrained himself to shoot with his other hand and his other eye. Unheard of! Not only did he stay in the SEALs, but he went on to be accepted into the most elite team of the most elite group of warriors in the world: SEAL Team Six."

"Where is Adam now?"

"He was killed in Afghanistan, but not before he became one of America's greatest warriors, taking out some of the top leaders in the Al Qaeda, all while organizing shoes from America to be sent over for hundreds of Afghani children. He never measured the cost of any mission, or of serving Afghani refugees who would never be able to repay his service. Adam once said, 'Life is not a journey to the grave with the intention of arriving safely in a pretty and preserved body, but rather to skid in broadside, thoroughly used up, totally worn out, and loudly proclaiming: Wow—what a ride.' Adam was more afraid of letting his fear control him and keep him from serving others than he was of dying and leaving his wife and children behind." James was silent until adding, "We have to decide what is worth fighting for, losing our job over, and possibly even dying for! We can't measure the cost of everything we do in life. We have to fight through the fear, especially when it comes to love. Love is not a give-and-take equation. It must be given freely with nothing expected in return. I call it the hundred-hundred model. People want the relationship to be fifty-fifty, but you have to give a hundred percent without counting the risk or the cost. Love and serve the young men you have the opportunity to lead, regardless of whether they, their parents, or your administration appreciate you! If you only love while looking for love in return, it's not love."

Danny thought this over then said, "I'm not doing this job for a huge 'thanks', I just want a tiny bit of appreciation some days and not to be thrown out on my ass at the end of the year."

Reflect and write: What are some of your greatest fears and anxieties in life?

James, sensing Danny was starting to turn it around, said, "Love is unconditional and does not measure the cost and return. Give them everything, and you will be surprised by what happens."

As James talked, Danny looked around the campgrounds and noticed the snow getting thicker and thicker. "The snow is getting worse. It's not letting up at all. I'm starting to think we have a pretty slim chance of making the summit tomorrow. My future for next season doesn't look much better at this stage, but you're saying that I have to go all-in, commit to the process, and love my players the best I can. I appreciate the encouragement."

James looked directly into Danny's eyes. "Danny, I'm not here to encourage you. I'm here to remind you of what you already know. Every single action, inaction, response, and thought you find yourself having is simply a surfacing of awareness. These all live inside of you; you just need someone like me to remind you what you're made of. Surrendering the destination will help you to unlock these hidden and forgotten practices. Before you go to bed, try and surrender to your fears."

"How do I do that?"

"Create a list of your greatest fears and anxieties. Start with the first item on the list. Ask yourself, 'Will this matter in five years?' If the answer is *no*, then write it down on a piece of paper and throw that piece of paper into the fire. Now, ask yourself, 'What *will* matter in five years?' Then take one step toward something that will matter. If you're anxious about winning your conference championship, you might realize what really matters is the relationships the experience built, so you could organize a team event focused on building relationships outside of practice. Now, if the answer is *yes*, then list everything within your control. Acknowledge that, regardless of the outcome, you will still have an opportunity for growth through the experience. Finally, take action on one of the controllables. For example, if you're afraid of your players not respecting you, create a list of all the things that leaders do to gain respect. Start by taking action on one of those commitments. Do you think you can do that?"

Looking around once again, Danny responded, "Well, it's either that or sit here staring at the snow and letting my fear of not being able to climb drive me crazy. I'll give it a shot." Danny then rose up, tucked the blanket around his shoulders, and said goodnight to James.

"Have a good sleep, Danny. And don't forget that each snowflake will fall no matter how much you wish it didn't. Mother Nature answers to no one."

CHAPTER 10

THE PROCESS IS GREATER THAN RESULTS

Danny and James didn't have far to go, but the little distance they did have to travel would be harrowing. The snow was deep, and parts of the path were icy. Danny looked up and thought he could see the peak of the mountain, but as soon as they got close, he realized there was another peak ahead of him. As they continued to climb, Danny grew tired and doubted whether he could make it to the top.

As he grudgingly put one foot in front of the other, he longingly looked toward the summit. Losing focus at the beautiful scenery in front of him, Danny stepped on a patch of ice, slipped, and fell flat on his face. As he started to slide down the side of the mountain with nothing in sight to slow his descent, James reached out and grabbed him by the collar, once again pulling him to safety. Once they were both safe and settled, James smiled and said, "The mountain is trying to teach you yet another lesson! You focused on the destination, and you took your eyes off the path, much like a coach obsessed with the results!"

Danny's heart was still racing. For a second, he'd thought he was going to die, or at least get badly injured, which could have been a death sentence at that height. "You just saved my life!" They both sat down to catch their breath. "Thank you. Thank you for *all* you have done. I really haven't said that enough on this journey. Whether we reach the top or not, you have given me so much to think about when I go home."

James paused, as if to let the compliment soak in. "You're welcome, Danny. I'm truly grateful to have met you and spent time together. A long, long time ago, I came to climb this mountain as well, but I was on a one-way trip. I was practically homeless, addicted to drugs and alcohol, and I had hurt everyone who had ever loved me. I lied and stole to sustain my terrible drug habit. I left quite a path of destruction. But even then, I was pretty blessed. There was one guy who just wouldn't give up on me. He was really supportive, and he helped me find a rehab program. While I was in treatment, a group of us got to climb up this mountain. When you started your climb, you were wrestling with the question of whether to stay in coaching or not. When I started my climb, I had all but made up my mind to take my life during the climb."

"What happened? Why didn't you?"

"Just like Adam Brown, I found my passion and decided I could use my passion to fulfill my purpose, to transform my life and the lives of others. When I made the decision to live, I was pretty worried my family members wouldn't have me back, and some still haven't welcomed me back into their lives. It's hard, but I can't control it, so I must choose to let it go. The people in your life may choose to not believe or accept the positive changes and steps you take in your life, but don't let that stop you from moving forward. You just have to continue putting one step in front of the other."

Danny looked up and could see the summit only a few hundred feet in the distance. Keeping his eyes directly ahead and on the path, he started to climb with a new determination. Danny's heart started to race while they climbed the final few hundred feet. He was overcome by emotion. He had made it to the last few steps of his journey. He paused for a second, took a deep breath, and put his left foot in front of his right. Suddenly, the mountaintop leveled out and Danny found himself standing at the summit. As he planted both feet on the top of the mountain, he felt an immediate sense of relief. Looking all around him, it became very apparent why it was called Clearview Mountain; he could see for what felt like thousands of miles around him.

Danny pulled out his camera and took a selfie. He couldn't wait to share this on social media with his friends. He was so busy celebrating the moment and capturing as many shots as he could that he didn't even notice James come alongside him.

"An amazing view, isn't it?"

"It's beautiful. A postcard doesn't do it justice. I'm definitely going to get one of these pictures printed out and hang it on my wall."

"Danny, you know you could have just bought a really high-quality photo of a view from the summit, right? Why put up your photo instead of a professional photograph?"

"Because I'm the one that took the photo; it's personal and it has a meaningful story behind it. Looking at it will remind me of every challenge I had to overcome to reach the summit."

"Yep! And that is exactly why it's not about reaching the destination, it is about the experience and the journey. Our big goals, our desire for accomplishment, and the destination itself are not bad things, but they are meaningless without the experience. I'm so glad the destination means something to you because of the experience—the struggles you had to overcome to be here."

Danny continued to look around and saw another mountain not too far off in the distance. "What mountain is that?"

"That mountain," James said, pointing into the distance. "That mountain is Shadow Mountain. It's over fifteen hundred feet taller than Clearview Mountain."

"You've got to be kidding me! I thought I had climbed the tallest in the area."

James chuckled. "Danny, once you climb one peak, there will always be another one to climb, until you get to the tallest peak in the world— Mount Everest. Do you know how risky it is to climb a mountain like Everest? There are a lot of people who die trying. So don't spend any time comparing your accomplishment to another opportunity. Celebrate the joy you felt as you reached the summit but understand that joy will start to decline as soon as you get to the top and see another mountain, another challenge."

"Absolutely! I think that's one of the reasons I was such a success-ful player and a coach. I was never happy with what I achieved, I always wanted more—wanted to continue to raise the bar."

James nodded in approval. "And that's a good thing! But the problem comes when people feel that achieving more will fill some hole in their lives. Achievement only continues to spark a stronger desire to achieve more. But that can suck all the joy out of the experience. I call that the achievement trap."

"How do you avoid the achievement trap?" Danny asked.

"By keeping your focus on the process—the journey. Carli Lloyd is one of the greatest female soccer players to ever play the game. She wrote a book called *When Nobody Was Watching*. As a young player, she real-ized that striving for perfection could work for you and against you. Striv-ing for perfection or being *the best* will torment you. In her book, she says, 'You can make the journey hard and joyless if you never allow yourself a few moments of contentment because you are pushing so hard to do even better. This is the line I walk constantly.'[6] Later in her career, she started to find joy in the journey after intensive physical and mental training every day for over ten years, when others were busy sleeping and partying. She adopted a growth mindset and found fulfillment in the process." James looked at the view before adding, "She described her feelings after win-ning the World Cup in twenty-fifteen by saying, 'I do not want to stop here. I want to keep getting better and better. I don't want to be satisfied, ever. That may sound grim, but it isn't at all. It is joyful, because the pur-suit of progress is joyful.'"

"But what really changed for her?"

"She started to strive for progress, not perfection. She worked and competed to be *her* best, not *the* best. She redefined success. Apply that standard to your life, Danny. How do you define success in coaching?

6   *When Nobody Was Watching: My Hard-Fought Journey to the Top of the Soccer World* by Carli Lloyd

Even more important, on your deathbed, how do you want people to remember you?"

Enjoying the wonderful view from above, Danny sat down, taking in the view and the powerful lessons James had just shared. He was starting to understand much of what James imparted, which was causing a drastic shift in his beliefs. Even then, it was not always easy to be challenged like this. James was challenging the very beliefs and views Danny had held for much of his life. He had always loved John Wooden's definition of success: "A peace of mind knowing I did the very best I could to become the best I'm capable of becoming." But it wasn't *his* definition. He needed to craft his own definition. Danny pulled out his water bottle, took a large swig, then rummaged through his bag and pulled out his journal. As James sat and meditated on the summit, Danny took a few minutes to write.

My Definition of Success

Success is fulfilling my purpose, living by my values and principles.

How I Want to Be Remembered at the End of My Life

I want the people at my funeral to know I loved them.

I want people to talk about the positive difference I made in their lives and the world around them.

I want people to be glad and grateful to have known me.

Reflect and write: Take a moment to define success for you. What does it look like? What do you hope to leave behind for the world to enjoy?

Satisfied with his efforts, Danny shared his responses with James, who had a look of pride on his face. "What is your birth name?"

Puzzled, he responded hesitantly, "Daniel."

"Why do you go by Danny?"

"I guess I always thought it sounded cooler, but my mother still calls me Daniel."

"Do you know what Daniel means?"

"Not really."

"It's Hebrew. It means 'God is my judge.' A powerful name and a great reminder for yourself as you move forward. As you change the way you coach, the way you parent, and the way you love others, people will criticize you and try to tear you down. People will not want to believe you are capable of changing, because it will make them feel guilty. Guilty that they are unwilling to change themselves. Do not let the criticism of others deter you from the process of becoming your best self."

"Daniel," Danny said aloud. "I'm going to start going by Daniel again. Not only will my mother be excited, but it will be a symbol of my change!"

James smiled. "Well, Daniel, you can change your name and you may even feel you have been changed through your experience this week. But it will be similar to when you watch a powerful movie or read an inspiring book or listen to a motivational speaker. It will be a lot of hype and feeling, but not much will have really changed when you wake up the next morning. You will go back to work pumped up and ready to go, but then you'll realize your circumstances have not changed. You will realize your condition has not changed, as you will still have days where you are angry, sad, and feel empty." James shifted his position. "A transformation of being cannot happen without action. Not until you consistently change the way you live will you develop habits necessary to experience real growth as a person. The hard part is that most people don't change until they hit rock bottom. As Dr. Henry Cloud says, 'We change our behavior when the pain of staying the same becomes greater than the pain of changing. Consequences give us the pain that motivates us to change.' Are you willing to endure more of the same pain you have been experiencing? Do things need to get more painful and desperate before you start to transform the way you operate? I hope you don't wait until you are fired, lose your home, or get to the end of your life to start the transformational process."

Daniel stood up and looked out from the mountain. He was now seeing his world for what it could be, not just for what it was. So many challenges were waiting for him. He knew he had to decide if he were going to run and hide from those challenges or thrive on them. In some ways, the easiest thing to do would be to start over at a new school. It would almost be easier if he were fired. A new slate. Still, he knew this great challenge would be an incredible opportunity for growth if he chose to view it that way. He loved the young men he had the opportunity to coach, he loved the vision he had for the program, and he believed that love was greater than any of the challenges he would face.

"I'm in!" Daniel said with conviction.

"Well then, before we head home, you need to write your coaching manifesto."

"A coaching manifesto?" Daniel said, somewhat confused. "What is that?"

James looked in Daniel's direction and quickly responded, "A coaching manifesto is a declaration of who you are as a coach. When you create a manifesto, you outline your vision and your plan to execute that vision. It's a living document, something that should inspire you, guide you, and remind you of what is important to you. The key components of the manifesto are:

- **Mission**
- **Values**
- **Principles**
- **Standards of Behavior, Language, and Attitude**
- **Commitments**
- **Success Defined**

Even when times are tough, a coaching manifesto can guide you through the challenges you might face. Does that make sense?"

Daniel smiled. "Absolutely. I want to get started on it right away."

For a step-by-step guide to building your manifesto, go to thriveonchallenge.com to download the Calling Up Coach's Guide.

PART II
THE PROCESS STARTS WITH YOU

You certainly might feel as if you are going somewhere in life, but there is a gap between where you are and where you want to be. Can you feel the tension? Once you create a clear vision, it can be tempting to try and change others to align with you. However, don't get ahead of yourself. You have to take the first step, and we cannot call others up until we take that first step.

In Part II of this book, Daniel feels a little overwhelmed by the distance between where and who he is and where and who he wants to be. This happens to us all at one point in time. And sometimes, it can be so overwhelming that we look for quick fixes or "shortcuts." When those don't work, we just give up.

Start small and stay consistent. Slow and steady. Part II will share many small actions that you can do consistently to build good habits. It's unlikely that anyone could implement all of them at once, but it is paramount to identify what is essential and what works for you.

CHAPTER 11

THE MOST INFLUENTIAL LEADER

Daniel walked his oversized golden retriever down the street. He enjoyed these long walks, as it allowed him to reflect on the day's challenges and consider his responses and how he could better resolve the issues he regularly faced. But tonight was different. Daniel was fuming on this cold April night, after a disastrous end-of-the-year banquet with the team. He could only think about one thing in that moment: *Why did I decide to come back?*

He wanted to scream but was worried the neighbors would think he was totally crazy. He wanted so badly to tell off every single one of those ungrateful players and their parents. He was already sick of it, and it had only been two weeks since his fateful journey up Clearview Mountain.

All the positive feelings and energy had quickly been depleted over the last week of work. Daniel had worked tirelessly preparing for a great meal, passing out awards, and crafting speeches to share positive things about each player on the team. He had spent countless hours reviewing video recordings to put together highlights with every player on the team. He had even prepared what he thought was a great speech about his mission as a coach moving forward! It took him a lot of time to get ready for this event, and only became more complicated when parents failed to communicate how many people were coming, who was paying for their meals in advance, and even what they wanted to eat! It was just a logistical nightmare.

Daniel had worked up the energy to push forward and do his best to have a great end-of-the-season experience. But the banquet could not have gone any worse for Danny. Families arrived late, some didn't even show, and others openly complained about their food, their table, and the poor service from the restaurant hosting the event. Daniel struggled to get through the two hours with a smile on his face, but he somehow managed.

As he wrapped up the evening, he silently hoped this would be the year a parent or a player stood up and thanked him for all his effort—maybe even give him a small gift as a token of their appreciation. Instead, parents and players could not have been in a bigger hurry to get out of there. They awkwardly passed right by the coaching staff with no more than a "have a good night." Finally, a player named Brian and his parents came over to him, shook his hand, and said "thank you." Brian was on the junior varsity team, but he barely ever played. Still, he let all the coaches know what a great year it was for him and that he was grateful for the opportunity. After that, there was just Daniel, left all by himself to clean up.

As Daniel packed up his things, he felt a pain deep in his chest and struggled to hold back tears. *Four years . . . four years and nobody cares. Even if I'm the worst coach ever, I don't deserve this, and I'm definitely not the worst coach ever. The more I sacrifice, the more I give, the more painful this is!*

As Daniel drove home, his wife called him to ask how things went.

"Horrible. Absolutely horrible. No different than any other year."

"I'm sorry. I appreciate all you do for those boys, and someday they may learn to appreciate it as well." Brownie—his nickname for her—was always so kind and empathetic toward his challenges. Even so, it didn't make him feel any better.

As Daniel pulled into the garage, he checked his phone to see the time. 10:14 p.m. Another night away from his family, not seeing his wife, kids, or catching his favorite shows on TV. Suddenly, he saw two unread text messages and an unread email.

The first text read: *Really, coach?* Jayden *is your starting player for four years and he doesn't get the MVP award?*

The second text read: *Daniel, we are really disappointed that Grayson did not get an award. Four years in the program, he sacrificed countless hours and never complained. Surely you could have found some way to acknowledge that other than a few words in your speech.*

The email came from another disgruntled parent, and it had clearly taken them the last hour to craft. The email started: *Coach, I have never been the type of parent to say something, but I cannot hold my tongue any longer...*

The parent outlined every complaint he had about the season, from his son's playing time to the attitudes of the other kids, the poor offensive strategy, the selfish culture, the horrible banquet food, and how his son only had one clip in the entire highlights video. The email finished with:

Please do not mention this to David, as he would be incredibly embarrassed if he knew I contacted you. The sad part for Daniel was that none of this was new to him. It was the same old stuff, just a different day.

Now he was out walking the dog in the freezing cold, trying to think about the things he was grateful for while simultaneously reminding himself of his purpose for coaching in the first place. It wasn't particularly helpful, and he kept getting angrier and angrier. He felt so far away from being the coach he wanted to be and having a positive impact on others. He knew he wasn't supposed to be focused on his destination, but he couldn't help it.

As he walked back home, in a hurry to get out of the cold and into bed, he heard a faint groan off the path in the park near his house. He slowed down and recognized a person struggling. His dog tugged at him to investigate, so he backtracked to a side trail through the park. He found an elderly man flat on his back, struggling to get up.

Daniel ran over to the man. "Hey! Hold on. Don't get up. Are you okay? What happened?"

The elderly man looked up at Daniel. "Thank the Lord! I was lying here praying someone would come along. I slipped and fell on this black ice and haven't been able to get up for the last five minutes. In the middle of April. Who would have thought there'd be ice on the ground?"

"Can you move? Are you in pain? Let me call nine-one-one."

"No, I'm okay. Just old and not as strong as I used to be. Ninety-nine years of age and flat on my back on a freezing night in the park. I'm lucky you made it to me, or I wouldn't have made it to a hundred! Can you please help me up?"

Daniel helped him up and asked him where he lived. Realizing he was only two houses down from his house, he agreed to walk him all the way home and get him settled. He was embarrassed that he had never noticed the elderly man, as they had been living next to each other for the last four years.

As they got to his door, Daniel asked for his name.

"My name is John. Daniel, would you like to join me for a cup of tea?"

"Wait, how do you know my name?"

John smiled. "I know everyone's name around here. I see you with your beautiful children and wife. I've followed you and your team for the last four years at Washington Prep. Actually, I have had the opportunity of watching you coach a few games. Now, will you join me for a quick cup of tea before bed?"

Daniel hesitated, really desirous to get home and get some sleep. He didn't really see much purpose in spending time with this old man, but he relented. "Sure."

Once inside the small house, John motioned for Daniel to take a seat at his kitchen table and started to prepare the tea. While doing so, he asked Daniel, "Isn't it late at night for you to be out walking the dog?"

"I should be asking you the same thing! We had our end-of-the-year awards banquet tonight, and I needed to cool off."

"Cool off?"

"Yeah, it was a disaster. A long story that you probably don't have any interest in hearing."

John sat back in his recliner and locked eyes with Daniel's. Inwardly, Daniel felt that John wanted more than anything in the world to hear his story, and was compelled to keep going. Over the next hour, Daniel poured everything out. He told John about the disastrous awards night, his goals and hopes when he came to Washington Prep, his job being on the line, the ungrateful players and parents, and even his journey up Clearview Mountain a few weeks earlier.

John listened intently to every word. Without realizing it, Daniel felt safe and ended up sharing way more than he would with even his good friends. Full of empathy, John asked Daniel, "Do you model the love and character that you expect from those you lead?"

Daniel thought about the answer and felt embarrassed. "Well, I mean, I think I do a pretty good job. I really do try hard to talk about character, and I demand that they work hard and be respectful."

John sat forward in his chair. "Back in my days as a coach, I realized pretty early on that giving them handouts or talking about character was meaningless if they didn't see evidence of my character in the way I operated as a coach, leader, and even a husband and father. I learned that, in coaching, your own personal example is one of the most powerful leadership tools you possess. Be what you want your team to become."

Daniel nodded. "I didn't realize you were a coach!"

"I never saw myself as a 'coach,' I always saw myself as a teacher. I was far from perfect and never tried to be perfect, just better every day. I even used to smoke, but one day, I realized that my example wasn't the *biggest* thing influencing those I led; it was the *only* thing! So, I quit smoking. I'm ninety-nine years old now, and I'm still trying to be a little better every day."

"Ninety-nine years old. You must have some incredible stories!"

"We *all* have stories. And the stories we live are powerful. How have we lived? How are we living right now? Sadly, our behaviors don't always match up to our aspirations for others. People in positions of power who want others to 'behave' should first reflect on how they behave themselves! If you can't model the virtues you claim to value, how do you expect your players to?"

Daniel now felt a little defensive. "I know I have a lot of room to improve, but I'm nowhere near as screwed-up or lost as these people. I work hard, and I have a good attitude most of the time. I'm just trying to help other people; it's my purpose—my mission!"

"And it's an admirable mission. Daniel, we need more coaches with your vision. I had a very similar vision in my years as a coach, but I always had to be careful. If I was in a position to see others' faults more clearly than my own, I became a hypocrite. The best way for me to serve my players and help them with their issues was for me to address my own issues! I had to be a model for them to follow, not some coaching-mechanic trying to 'fix' people."

Daniel nodded. "But I don't think you get it. All these people do is complain and look at my faults as a coach. Parents, players, fans, and administrators are so critical; they never look within."

"It isn't easy to learn from criticism, but it comes when we don't learn from other methods. If we're not open to what others may try to tell us kindly, we are going to face it later in a much more difficult way. You don't need to accept their judgment of you as a person, but you should listen to their criticism. The writer Dr. James Richards suggests we ask, 'What is it in my behavior that makes them reach this judgment about me?'"

As John stoked the fireplace, Daniel sat in silent thought. He had tried to develop character in his players and felt he'd made it the core of his program. He'd even paid money from his own salary to cover the cost of a motivational speaker to come in and give a talk on character. He'd paid for a leadership program that they did once a week as a team. He really believed he'd valued leadership. But suddenly, he was facing some hard questions: *How many of the leadership qualities that we discussed each week did I truly demonstrate? And am I okay with these young men emulating my leadership?*

The more he mulled this over, the more he realized he seemed to have a much different standard of what leadership and character should look like for himself than what it should look like for his players.

John looked at Daniel and asked, "Who is the most influential leader on your team?"

Daniel quietly said, "Well, I used to think it was Jayden, and I blamed his poor leadership for our problems. The truth is, I'm the most influential leader on the team. I don't need to look any further than myself to see where the leadership breakdown begins. Paying for some motivational speaker and a leadership program and even talking to them about character is like throwing seeds on the blacktop during a hot summer day and expecting them to take root. I haven't built a culture, and I haven't modeled the willingness to change and grow."

> **Reflect and write: Do you model the love and character you expect from those you lead? If so, how do you do that? If not, what can you do to ensure you make it a priority?**

John put his arm on Daniel's shoulder. "Focus on becoming a better version of yourself every day. It all starts with you. After some time, people are going to want what you have, and you will inspire them. Imagine you're flying on an airplane, holding your one-year-old son, and the plane suddenly experiences a loss of cabin pressure and appears to be headed for an emergency landing. What are you supposed to do first?"

"Put on my oxygen mask!"

"What do you think your first inclination would be?"

"Put on my son's mask!"

"Exactly, it's a natural urge to want to 'fix' and 'take care of others' first, but we have to put our own mask on before we can help others. We have to have the courage to go first."

"Thank you, John." Daniel hesitated, about to ask a question, but he was worried that John would say no. Finally, he worked up the courage to ask, "John, you seem to have a lot of great wisdom and experience in coaching. Would you be up for having tea with me more often? Maybe I could come by once a week, and we can talk? I've been looking for some-one to help me along the path for some time now, and I think you could really help me help myself!"

"I'd be glad to, Daniel. Let's plan on meeting once a week!"

"Thank you!" Daniel didn't know who this John was, but he knew he came into his life for a reason. He was so encouraged to have someone new to help him along the path, like James had helped him climb the mountain. Daniel began the short walk home, thankful he had met John. It didn't change his feelings about his team or the banquet that evening, but it gave him hope that better days might be ahead.

CHAPTER 12
YOUR LIMITING BELIEFS

Daniel felt quite lucky, as he had missed interactions like this one with John. James set a high threshold for mentorship and guidance, and John seemed to have the same demeanor and wisdom to share. It was just what Daniel needed, and he felt a new energy during the week! He once again focused on his commitments to reading, reflecting, and journaling every day, which he had fallen away from only a few days after returning from Clearview Mountain. But John inadvertently reminded him of its importance, and he rededicated himself to this daily practice.

The two agreed to meet again the following Saturday, and Daniel awaited the meeting with eager anticipation. Saturday proved to be a beautiful day outside, and John asked Daniel to take him to the aquarium to get out of his home. John loved to sit and watch the fish, and he visited often with his many grandchildren. It wasn't a long drive to the oversized fishbowl, and they parked near the front of the parking deck. They approached the front, and Daniel bought them two tickets, insisting on covering the cost. As they walked through the aquarium, they came upon a tank full of small minnows and large fish called the wall-eyed pike, where an aquarist was tossing in food pellets to feed the fish.

John asked, "Daniel, did you know that the wall-eyed pike only eats other little fish in the wild? But when they bring it to an aquarium they have to train it to not eat the other fish?"

"Seriously?" Daniel responded.

"Yup. Pretty interesting, right? To do this, they put it in a tank with minnows, but they slide a plate of glass into the tank to separate the minnows from the pike. The pike obviously doesn't see the glass, and repeatedly swims into it in their hunt for the little guys. They eventually give up. When they do, the aquarists can pull the glass. The pike won't eat the minnows—they are conditioned to believe they can't catch them. If the aquarists didn't feed them, the pike would actually *starve*! This is a lot like coaching! We hold certain beliefs that starve us from more beneficial ways of doing things. Our beliefs limit our power and ability to help transform the lives of the people we lead. These fish don't realize it, but there is better food out there. Just like we don't realize there is a better way."

Daniel replied, "Like the story *Moneyball*? Great book! It was crazy to think that the owners, managers, and scouts held onto this flawed belief system about talent and potential for a long time. They were held back by how much they could pay a player. Billy Beane was the first general manager to break free from those beliefs and try a whole new way of evaluating talent."

"Exactly! Except we have limiting beliefs in nearly every aspect of coaching, not just when it comes to evaluating talent. We hold onto those beliefs because to go against them would be terrifying and leave us open to criticism from others. Except in life, the leaders who're able to change the world are the ones who're crazy enough to go against the crowd. They buck the trends and do what they think is right without care for the opinion of others. They see things as they truly are, not as they wish them to be!"

Daniel nodded excitedly. "That's one of the reasons I loved reading and journaling so much this week. I'm learning something new every day, and I'm really able to reflect on some of the things I have believed about coaching for so long. I know I need to break free from those limiting beliefs. They are hurting my progress and development. In one of my books, I read about a study where researchers looked at horse betting. They interviewed people before and after making a bet on a horse. They discovered that people became nearly forty percent more confident about a decision just because they had already made it. They had no reason to be more confident other than their investment in that choice. That speaks volumes to me. We support a decision as being right just because we are the one making it."

John smiled and affirmed Daniel. "I'm glad to see you're reading like that! There are just so many great mentors found within the pages of books."

Daniel was excited to share even more of what he had read. "It's incredible! There are studies out there that show that when we form strong beliefs, it causes activity in the brain that puts us in a mental state where we only see what we have predetermined. Our brain literally selects what information we see to confirm our beliefs and perception and ignore data that goes against our perception. I read that our brains are a hundred thousand times more powerful than the body's sensors, which means we experience a far different world than the real one. It's scary, because I have realized my mind doesn't seek the truth, it just wants to validate my perceptions even more. That's really part of what's limiting me from moving forward, I think."

As John walked through the exhibits in the aquarium, he asked Daniel for help up some steps, still sore from the fall earlier in the week. Daniel continued, "The great part about these books is that the research really connects with the experiences of the great coaches I'm reading about. The crazy part is that science and experience know that leadership in sports and business should look a lot different than they currently do! It's actually criminal that we fail to develop as professionals, me included. If a doctor advanced and developed as little as a coach does, he would probably be sued for malpractice!"

Reflect and write: When was a time you realized you did something in the wrong way? How did that hurt your overall development and progression? Looking back, what could you have done differently to realize a better outcome?

John nodded. "I'm proud of you, because you are stepping outside your sport to learn new approaches and are already challenging the way we lead as a society. I spent my lifetime learning as much as I could, and now I try to pass it along to others just like you. Are you asking the right questions? That's the power of writing things down and having the opportunity to review them each and every day of your life. We look for a book or a mentor with all the right answers, but we really need to make sure we are asking the right questions in the first place. One question is: How does this relate to my behaviors and beliefs as a coach? Asking better questions leads us to better solutions. The principles and tools you read about are just that—principles and tools. How we apply them is the art of coaching! It's not a science. Words without action is really just a bunch of nothing."

"One of the differences between good and great is that when people start to achieve things, they stop asking the important questions. We must be humble enough to ask repeatedly: How can I do this better? If you aren't doing that every single day of your life, then you're just setting yourself up for failure."

Daniel understood John's point and felt like he was starting to connect the dots. "I remember in my time with James, we talked about the importance of a growth mindset. He talked to me about Carol Dweck, who uncovered in her research that it's people's belief system that shapes what they are most able to achieve. By just teaching people the difference between a growth mindset and a fixed mindset, you help them move more toward a growth mindset. Our beliefs about abilities and potential—she calls them 'self theories'—decide how we see our experiences and limit what we're able to accomplish. It's really powerful stuff."

John turned toward Daniel. "Precisely! Now it's time for you to start investigating those beliefs. Leave no stone unturned! Many of the beliefs you investigate are going to be very uncomfortable to change, because acknowledging that the way you have been doing things wasn't the best way is going to take vulnerability on your part. You know what—here's what I would try to do to really explore this concept. When you go home tonight, pick a couple areas of your leadership in which you think you might need growth. Ask yourself, 'How can I do this better?' Then write down your answers. Maybe we can talk about those the next time we meet."

As the two walked into the exhibit labeled "Deep Sea," Daniel was immediately taken aback by the wide array of different sized fish. They were all types of beautiful colors, covering every shade of the rainbow. He then focused on one fish, which a poster on the wall informed him was a grouper. The fish was huge and looked old and wise to him. He quietly laughed, thinking that it reminded him of his wonderful mentors. Daniel wondered if perhaps the grouper would offer him some helpful advice if he stared at it long enough.

CHAPTER 13

THE IMPACT OF YOUR EXPERIENCES

One Saturday evening, after Daniel had put his children to bed, he drove over to John's house to take him out for dinner. He had no idea where they were going. John gave directions to a hole-in-the-wall Italian restaurant where everyone seemed to know him. Daniel was eager to get the conversation started and learn more about coaching, but they spent the first few hours eating a five-course Italian dinner and discussing family, social issues, and life. John seemed more interested in knowing about his personal life than talking about coaching. After a lengthy dinner, John invited Daniel on a walk around the neighborhood to "work off some of the dinner."

As they were walking along, John asked, "Daniel, can you tell me about your high school coach? He seems to have played a big part in your life."

Daniel hesitated, unsure how to describe his coach. "Well, I think he was a good man, or at least, he tried to be, but he made me hate basketball. He was a yeller and a screamer. Every time I made a mistake or failed to give a hundred percent effort, he told me I was lazy, selfish, or stupid. And I wasn't mentally tough enough to handle it. Teammates and other fans told me I had to learn to block it out, but I couldn't. I didn't know how. I ended up becoming so depressed when I played poorly, because the harder I fought to stay afloat, the deeper I sank. Almost like I was in quicksand."

"How did others cope with your coach's style?"

"Some could hack it, some couldn't. People believed he was making men out of us, toughening us up, and if we quit, we were a sissy."

"What do you think?"

"I think it was who he was. He even shared with us that he had tried to change and be nicer, but he was unable to. Still, I know many people later went on to love and respect this coach."

"We never remember things the way they happened; we remember the way things made us feel. I'm sorry you experienced that as a young man." John shook his head in disappointment. "It's a baffling situation in our sporting culture. A coach's example is the single most important aspect of coaching. If you are unwilling to grow and change, then why would the people you lead ever believe they're capable of change?"

"That makes sense!" Daniel agreed.

John slowed down as they approached a park bench. Sitting down, he turned to Daniel and asked, "Have you ever asked yourself why you coach the way you do?"

"Not really. I guess I change and grow because I want to be the best coach I can be. I'm hard on players because I'm trying to push them to be better."

"But why do you choose to be that way? Why do you believe pushing people to be better or being hard on them is the most beneficial way?" John asked without taking his eyes off Daniel.

"I guess it's the only way I know how to coach. We learn how to coach by watching how we were coached."

"I agree," John said. "When you examine your beliefs about coaching and past behaviors, it's important to remember that ninety-nine percent of people are doing the best they can with what they know; they typically just don't know any better. Our brains are conditioned to create distractions from problems we are afraid to address. One of the problems in your own coaching is that it's greatly influenced by those who have coached you. If you want to change the way you coach, you need to understand your experiences of being coached. Those negative experiences can be your story as a coach or they can help you understand and empathize with yourself and the young people you lead."

Daniel nodded; he had already given some thought to how his experience as a player related to his experience as a coach. "As a player, the more I achieved, the more I found my value in my performance. It really made me miserable and start to hate basketball. Later on, when I started coaching, I loved the experience of helping the young people I was coaching, and I think I was coaching for all the right reasons. But just like when I was a player, the more success I experienced, the more I tied my value as a coach to my performance. Suddenly, I was coaching to protect my identity, and I became more insecure. I felt insignificant and embarrassed after every loss. I couldn't handle losing, because I thought it said something about me as a person."

"Sadly, this is the message our sporting culture sends to players from a very early age: being a man is about winning, dominating, and controlling others. Nothing about respecting, empowering, and loving others. So many coaches emasculate young men, and people praise them for it." John looked out over the park, which was lit up by the moon, then said with a sigh, "We have control over our explanations of our experiences, not our experiences themselves. What happened to you as a player and what you have done as a coach—those things are in the past. What's important is that you use those experiences to shape a positive perspective of what good coaching is."

Daniel was puzzled as to how this mattered. "I understand what you're saying, but how do I use that to become a better coach?"

"Start to rewrite your story! Stop being the victim of your past, and start using your past to shape the story of a man who becomes the coach he always wanted to be."

"Again . . . great, but how do I manage to do that?"

"There are two ways to get started: first, build a new circle of people—which is much easier in today's technological age—who will stretch, challenge, and model growth. If you only surround yourself with the same ideas and people, nothing new will ever permeate your world. You will never be challenged to examine your thinking, and you will walk around ignorant like so many others who are unwilling to reflect on the way they operate. Secondly, train! Train your behaviors. We can train our thoughts, beliefs, and attitudes through a process called cognitive behavioral therapy. Start by visualizing in your mind—or even writing out—how you will operate when faced with certain challenges. It's in this way we can retrain our default mode of operation." There was a moment of silence until John said, "I remember you sharing with me various principles from your coaching manifesto. Continue to use those principles to evaluate the way you're operating. But I want to share a new principle with you that was incredibly beneficial to me as a coach when reflecting."

> **Reflect and write: What are some of the beliefs and behaviors you could purge to evolve into a transformational coach?**

Daniel pulled out a pen and his little notebook, eager for the new principle.

John continued, "Effective does not always equal beneficial. What this means is that just because something is effective does not mean that it will be beneficial for the person. Starving yourself will lead to weight loss, but it is not a beneficial way to lose weight! Screaming, punishing, and controlling players can lead to more wins, but it will not develop character and leadership. Likewise, just because something is beneficial does not mean it will produce the effects we want. Healthy eating and exercise may not lead to the quick, easy gains that diet pills or crazy crash diets claim to produce, but they have a greater possibility of being sustained in the long term, as well as cultivating a more positive sense of self-worth, and a longer life. The effects are often unseen for some time, but it is beneficial. The same is true in coaching; often, operating in a beneficial way doesn't get the quick results we want in our microwave culture, but it *will* develop a sustainable transformational culture."

Daniel's eyes lit up. "I get it! So, when I reflect on my coaching behaviors, I need to ask myself: Is this beneficial or just effective? I need to see how it aligns with my purpose and values."

"Yes, and you're still young with a bright future ahead of you. A great writer named Goethe once said, 'Hell begins the day God grants you the vision to see all that you could have done, should have done, and would have done, but did not do.' You're starting to ask the right questions and look in the right places. Just keep pushing ahead."

CHAPTER 14

CALLING UP

Daniel had just finished some grading one day after school when he decided to stop by the gym. Three of the most talented players for the Warriors—Eddie, Dennis, and Archie—had asked to get into the gym during the off-season to work on their game. Just over a month after the season had ended, Daniel was excited to see that they were motivated enough to get back in the gym and get an early start on the forthcoming season.

As Daniel approached the gym, he not only heard balls bouncing, but a lot of laughter and ruckus. Upon walking in, he saw them trying in vain to dunk the ball, while the others recorded the fruitless endeavor. It was apparent they didn't go to the gym to work on their game, but to goof off and make Snapchat videos. While Daniel was furious, he did his best to remain calm.

"Can I speak with you three—right now?" He said in a stern voice, holding back his anger. "What are you guys doing?"

The three boys looked at each other, seeing who would speak first. Eventually, Eddie spoke up. "We got some shots up and were working on our dunks after. What's the big deal?"

Daniel only grew more irritated. "You got up some shots? You couldn't have been in here more than fifteen minutes, and you're already goofing off. Seriously? You guys want to get better and win, but you aren't willing to put the time and work ethic into it. If you're just going to come in here and goof off, then stay the hell out of *my* gym."

The boys' heads dropped. They apparently understood his point, but they didn't see how just wanting to have some fun was such a bad thing. At least they were in the gym, they all silently thought. Where was everybody else? Nothing ever seemed good enough for Coach D.

"Sorry, Coach," they half-muttered. Daniel, sensing their insincerity, stormed out of the building.

Daniel was furious with the boys, but something had also bothered him about himself. He didn't feel like he'd handled the situation well at all, but he couldn't stand back and let them waste their time. He had a responsibility to be honest with them and tell them the truth. The reality was that the three of them were so far away from accomplishing their goals of playing college basketball, and he felt it was his responsibility to tell them just how much they were slacking. As he pulled into the driveway, he decided to stop by John's house to share his concerns.

Daniel rang the doorbell and heard someone call, "Come in!" As he walked into the living room, he saw John sitting with another older man, though not as old as John.

"Daniel! Great to see you, though unexpected," John said.

"Sorry, I didn't realize you had company; I can come another time."

The other man spoke up. "Nonsense. John and I just finished up a great lunch. He's told me a great deal about you, and I'm excited to meet you. My name is Tony." Tony extended his hand and made eye contact with Daniel.

"Great to meet you, Tony. Thanks for sharing John with me today."

"Tell me, what brings you by today?" John asked. "You look a little distraught."

Daniel told John and Tony every part of the afternoon's story, even about feeling unsure how to handle the situation. "I just don't know what to do! I feel like I always have to play the bad guy or police their behavior. They just can't seem to make the right choices, and every time I think I'm getting through to them, they let me down."

John nodded at Tony with a look that said, *you take this one*. Tony smiled and asked Daniel, "What do Martin Luther King, Jr., Gandhi, Nelson Mandela, and Mother Teresa have in common?"

After some thought, Daniel replied, "I guess it's that they were all amazing people who inspired others regardless of their religion, race, or views. They really moved millions of people to action and to stand up for what they believe in."

"Why were their messages so inspiring?"

Daniel thought for a few seconds. "I'm not sure. Maybe because they were able to communicate challenging messages in such a positive way?"

Tony nodded and leaned close to Daniel, as if to tell him something very important. "They called people *up*, not out."

Daniel thought hard, mulling over Tony's words. It hit him like a bolt of lightning. It made so much sense, but he couldn't explain why.

Tony continued, "*Calling out* is defined as 'being summoned' or 'to challenge to a duel.' When we call people out, we're asking them for a fight! Critics call people out. People who believe they are superior call people out. It's negative in a sense. It's judgmental. It's about 'fixing' others. It's not about moving them to action and working to make a difference in their lives. *Calling up* is defined as 'to summon together, as for a united effort' or 'to bring forward for consideration or action.' Think about the difference between the two terms. There's a pretty important distinction. Leaders call people up. Leaders know we all struggle and fall short. It is positive. It is a promotion. It is seeing the good in others. It is inviting people on the journey to become a better version of themselves."

Daniel sighed. "That is exactly the type of leader I want to be, but it just doesn't come naturally to me at all, and I only seem to keep making mistakes. I get upset, and I react."

Tony smiled. "We all make mistakes in this world, but it's the people who learn and grow from their mistakes who are the most successful."

John, who had been listening intently, turned to Daniel. "Success is more likely when love is present in your heart for the people who make your organization a real team, that is, a family.[7] Why do so many people call others out? Because calling people out *can* be effective. Through fear, you are able to exercise some control over other people. But in turn, that's how they respond to you. They do things not because they want to, but because they want to avoid the consequences if they don't. You're angry when you work hard to improve, and you don't see the people in your organization working hard right there with you. It's okay to be angry when others let us down, but it's not beneficial to withdraw our love from them and try to control them at the same time."

Tony chimed in, "We can change ourselves, but we can't change others. We can only help them become better versions of themselves if they are willing and able to do so. It doesn't matter how hard you push them. You'll get nowhere if they're pushing you back."

Daniel threw his hands in the air, frustrated. "So, I'm just supposed to sit back and let them give no effort and accept that they're fine with being lazy?"

Tony smiled. "Daniel, there's a big difference between empathy and apathy. Empathy is about *understanding* what they are feeling or experiencing. Apathy is a lack of caring or feeling toward someone else and their actions. Apathy tolerates and accepts their actions."

Tony looked to John, who added, "Yes, people need to be held accountable for their actions, but we can still practice empathy in the process."

Daniel nodded in understanding. "I once heard true empathy is walking with their feet, not just in their shoes. It's the best way to see the world through their eyes. All three of those boys grew up in far worse circumstances than I did. It's not excusable, but I guess it is understandable that they don't have the work ethic that I had. I get so focused on the *opportunities* they have in life, with access to a gym, a coach who is always willing to work with them, and other things that many players would die for. But the truth is they don't have the *role models* or *examples* that I had growing up. So how do I move from being a critic to a leader? It doesn't sound like I can just snap my fingers and accomplish that."

---

7   *Wooden on Leadership* by John Wooden

John replied, "That's a great question. Communication is important. If you want to be a transformational leader—if you want to call people up—it takes a high standard of communication, both verbal and with your body language. That's one of the things those amazing leaders Tony mentioned had in common. They were remarkable communicators, able to reach people from all different walks of life."

Reflect and write: Who is the most inspirational leader in your life? How do they call up others?

Tony chimed in, "Alfie Kohn, one of the leading authors and speakers on parenting, education, and behavior, says, 'Better than yelling is telling. Better than telling is explaining. Better than explaining is discussing.' The challenge in coaching, teaching, and even parenting is that we know we have a responsibility not to tell others what they want to hear, but what they *need* to hear. The problem is, we don't do it in a beneficial way that will lead to their learning and growing from the feedback. I guess you could say it's kind of a catch twenty-two."

The light bulbs continued to illuminate in Daniel's head. He added, "John, it's just like what we talked about last week. A leader's job isn't to fix, but to serve. We need more role models, not critics. So, after I model what I claim to value, then what? How do I start to communicate?"

John chuckled. "Start by speaking softly and making suggestions, not demands. That's what the great leaders do so well."

Tony stood up as he readied to leave. "As leaders, we need to lead with love, not fear! As the author Dr. James Richards says, 'If anything will work, love will. If love will not work, nothing will.' How committed are you to making sure the people you lead feel loved? Raising the standard of your communication starts with love. Stop telling them where they need to go as people; lead them there!"

John smiled and got up from his oversized chair as well. "Great point, Tony. If we are to lead them there, we have to go first. We have to be willing to share our journey, so young people know they're not alone in the struggle. Too many people in this world sit on the sidelines, throwing criticism and judgment around, but are unwilling to be vulnerable. You can't lead without the strength of vulnerability."

Daniel, putting on his jacket, said, "Vulnerability doesn't sound much like strength to me!"

John chuckled. "This is probably a conversation for the next time we meet, Daniel. But try this and see if it helps. Go find those three players you just chewed out, and ask each of them the following question: How does it feel to be coached by me? Tell them you want to grow as a leader and ask them what you can do to make them feel more empowered. Use this information to identify the things you need to keep doing, start doing, and stop doing. If you do that, you'll be showing the real strength in vulnerability."

CHAPTER 15

THE POWER OF VULNERABILITY

D aniel spent the rest of the week trying to call up not just his players and students, but even his wife. He devised a very simple checklist before speaking to each of them:

1. Do I model the right behavior or virtue?

Only if he could say yes to number one would he go on to two and three.

2. Speak softly and use warm body language.
3. Ask or suggest how they might say or do something different next time.

Just this small change in his actions started to take some people by surprise. When he would ask to speak to a student or player, he realized they would almost immediately tense up. But in many cases, after he just lowered his voice, made eye contact, and smiled, he could sense a change in how people were receiving his feedback. This whole thing was starting to work.

Still, some people were not buying it. Two players in particular—Archie and Kevin—almost ran the other way when they saw him coming. They had a strained relationship with their coach since last season, when they both walked out of a pre-season practice and joined the bowling team just to get out of conditioning. It was absolutely inexcusable for the players to do this, and the administration did nothing to step up and support Daniel. But even then, Daniel had responded poorly to their immature decision. He publicly embarrassed the players and called them out in front of the whole team. Reflecting back on the experience, he knew he was leading with fear as he tried to teach them a lesson.

After dinner and getting the kids to sleep, Daniel sat down on the couch, staring off into space, worried about how to fix the relationship with Archie and Kevin. It seemed there was nothing he could do. Daniel's wife, Brownie, sat down next to him. With a concerned look on her face, Brownie asked, "You've been on another planet tonight, quiet and withdrawn. I know something is up. What's on your mind?"

"Oh, just Archie and Kevin."

"What's going on with those two now?"

"Oh, nothing new, just wondering how I can save the relationship. I used to be pretty close to them and felt respected, but ever since last year's fiasco, I think the relationship is all but dead. I screwed up. I *know* I screwed up. I mean, what they did was wrong, but I'm the coach, the adult, and the leader. I acted like an idiot. Like a total child."

Brownie asked, "Well, have you told *them* that?"

"Are you serious?! Leaders need to show strength, not weakness. If I told them that, they would totally lose all respect for me."

"I'm sorry to be the one to tell you this, but from what you tell me, it seems like they *currently* don't have much respect for you anyway. What do you really have to lose here?" Brownie paused then asked, "Let me ask you something. What do you think of when you hear the word 'vulnerability?'"

"Scared. Afraid. In a corner. Weak, I guess."

Brownie was a social worker who was able to build relationships with people from some of the roughest backgrounds. This was her area of expertise, so she was excited to share some of her professional training with her husband. "Daniel, I want you to think of the following circumstances:

Being the first to say, 'I love you.'

Asking me for help.

Interviewing for a big coaching job.

Speaking in front of a room full of people.

Taking the game-winning shot.

Apologizing for having done something wrong.

Do those take fear or courage? Do they take weakness or strength?"

Daniel immediately replied, "Courage and strength, definitely."

"Well, don't they also require vulnerability? I might not have said, 'I love you' back, and I could have laughed at you for needing help. You could fail to get the big job and mess up when speaking to a room full of people. You could miss the game-winning shot. And when you apologize, the other person could choose not to forgive you, right?"

Daniel nodded. "We are vulnerable to people's criticism and judgment, but you're right . . . it takes courage and strength to be vulnerable. I never thought of it that way."

"Yep, in fact, the more you try to shield yourself from vulnerability, the more afraid you will be of being seen, judged, and even failing." Brownie looked at Daniel's face as she said this, but he responded by staring at the ground, unwilling to make eye contact.

Daniel muttered, "I just don't do vulnerability. No offense, but I think it's more of a thing for women."

Brownie smiled. "You can't avoid vulnerability; eventually, it will always catch up with you. Especially if you're a leader. Only you get to choose how you will respond to moments where you face criticism, failure, and embarrassment. It takes strength to be vulnerable by sharing your struggles and weaknesses, but society conditions us to see our weaknesses as defining. We are conditioned to never admit it. You want to repair the relationships? You want to build meaningful relationships? Just think about your best friends. They became powerful and meaningful relationships when you were willing to share your struggles and failures. Let those boys see that things aren't easy for you, that you fail, and that you know you have things to work on. When you let them see you for who you truly are, then you can have an authentic and meaningful relationship."

Daniel looked at Brownie and nodded. "I guess you're right." He understood what he had to do if he were going to have any hope at salvaging the relationship with Archie and Kevin, but he was unsure whether he had the courage to actually do it.

The next day, Daniel sought out Archie and Kevin. He found them shooting free throws in the gym. He sat on the bleachers, watched them for a few minutes, then during a water break invited Archie and Kevin to join him in his office adjacent to the gym. They grudgingly followed Daniel to his office, and he closed the door behind them. Instead of sitting behind his desk, he sat at a group of chairs with the two young men. It was very clear they were nervous, and not excited about having to speak with him.

"I'll keep this short, because I want to respect your time. First, I want to apologize for the way I handled the situation last fall, when you both decided to join the bowling team. Regardless of whether what you did was right or wrong, I never should have treated you in such a manner. I was threatening, cold, and controlling, and there is no excuse. I hope you can forgive me for that. Secondly, I wanted to share with you that I'm trying to grow as a leader. I recognize that I have a lot of room for growth! I hope you will be willing to support me by not only forgiving me for the times I fall short, but by being honest with me and sharing any issues or problems that come up."

Archie and Kevin looked a little uncomfortable. Kevin spoke first. "Thanks, Coach, and I'm sorry too; it wasn't right the way I did things, but I was afraid of how you would respond and so I just avoided it."

"Thanks, Kevin," Daniel said through a smile.

Archie leaned back in his chair and just gave a little shrug. "Yeah, we're cool. I'm over it, so it's no big deal. Not sure I will play next year anyway."

Daniel was disappointed in his response, but he tried to respect Archie's feelings. "I get your hesitation to believe things will get better. I hope you both will give me a second chance."

As the boys left the room, Daniel felt a weight drop off his shoulders. It was an exhausting task to appear to 'have it all together' and trying to prove he was a strong leader. By being vulnerable, he didn't have to prove anything and could just focus on loving his players instead. Daniel was excited to get home and share, not only with his wife but also with John, because he was coming over for dinner that night to meet his family.

> **Reflect and write: What are the areas where you work hard to show strength? What are the areas where you have doubts and weaknesses?**

After an amazing dinner and getting the kids down, John, Brownie, and Daniel sat on the front porch. Daniel was excited to share all he had learned about vulnerability from his reading in the last week. "Did you know that Dr. Elena Bordova, one of the top educational researchers, actually recommends that elementary teachers commit errors on purpose? She believes it's important for leaders to show that mistakes are part of the learning process and to model a growth mindset when handling their mistakes. Not only do leaders need to model their core values, but they need to model their struggles to live by those values."

Brownie smiled and turned to John, saying, "He's starting to get it now, isn't he?"

John replied, "Yes, he is! I think you made quite the impact on him earlier in the week." Turning to Daniel, he asked, "So how do you feel after being courageously vulnerable with your players?"

"Honestly?" Daniel asked. "I feel relieved and actually happier. Definitely feel like it was the first step in the right direction in my relationships with those two."

Brownie chimed in, "You know, when we hide our feelings from others, our blood pressure will actually rise during the conversation! We crave authenticity and vulnerability in our relationships."

"I know exactly why I'm afraid to share. If I'm honest and even vulnerable, it's because I feel inadequate as a coach. I try to project this image of having it together and being a strong leader all the time, but that's just a mask." Even as Daniel said it, he felt some relief.

John, looking at Daniel, said, "Sadly, our culture and your experiences in life have taught you that the only emotion 'tough' men show is anger. Compassion, empathy, and vulnerability are seen as weaknesses. So, what do we choose? We choose anger, because who wants to be seen as weak?"

"I think I have a new principle to guide me along my journey, that will help me call people up."

"What is that?" John asked.

"Lead with my strengths; connect through my weaknesses."

CHAPTER 16
SEE PEOPLE AS PEOPLE

aniel picked up John in his truck to head to a nearby park for their weekly walk. This had become a ritual for the two of them, and Daniel looked forward to not just the mandatory physical exercise, but also the mental stretch. John pushed him, intentionally or otherwise, to question his belief-system and completely survey how he reacted to particularly challenging situations.

Traffic was horrible this Saturday afternoon, and Daniel was getting frustrated quickly. Nobody was letting him in as he tried to pull onto the main road. John looked on as Daniel's anxiety and aggression simultaneously rose. An elderly lady finally slowed down, waving him in. Daniel gestured and half-shouted a thank you from his car, appreciative that she let him in. A few minutes later, he got stuck on a one-lane road behind a slow driver. This proved too much for him to handle.

"Come on, come on, come on! What's this person's deal? He's going ten under the speed limit! You've got to be kidding me." Daniel tailed the person in an effort to encourage him to speed up. Finally, the person turned right, allowing Daniel to pass. As he passed by, he honked his horn at the old man to voice his displeasure. They arrived at the park, and Daniel abruptly pulled into a parking spot, showing a sense of relief that they had made it there. He was noticeably perturbed and felt a sense of shame for acting the way he did in front of John. *Chalk it up to one more thing I have to work on,* he silently thought to himself.

As they started their walk through the park, Daniel shared his anxiety about the start of the three weeks of summer basketball. "Summer practices have never gone well! Kids have always been lazy, and I can never seem to get anything out of them."

John slowed his walk, looked at Daniel, and asked, "When you were driving earlier, did you see people or objects?"

"I don't know what you mean."

"The car in front of you—the cars blocking your path. Did you see that as an object in the road, or did you see the people in the cars?"

"I guess I just saw the car."

"Are your needs more important than the needs of others? Are you the only one that's in a hurry to get somewhere? This is an important lens through which we view people in the world. People or objects. Let's sit down for a few minutes and look deeper into this concept."

John directed them to a bench on the path. They sat down, and John shifted his body in Daniel's direction. "Get out your pen and notebook. I want you to write down the name of every player on your team."

> **Reflect and write: Write down the names of the people you lead and next to each name write down the first word that comes to mind.**

Daniel followed John's orders. After a few moments he had an extensive list of twelve players on the piece of lined paper. "Now, write down the first word that comes to mind when you think of this person." John spent the next two minutes writing, and after he finished, John said, "Read me those words."

Daniel sighed and then read the following words: "Lazy. Entitled. Silly. Fake. Goofy. Cold. Unrealistic. Leader. Soft. Ungrateful. Relaxed. Apathetic."

"I call this the 'heart posture test.' How do you view others? If you believe people are lazy or entitled, you're going to do things and look for things that will validate the way you see them. We have to change the way we view others. Until you change your heart posture—see people as people, value them for the good in them—you will be a transactional coach."

"So now I have to retrain my heart?"

"You betcha!"

John and Daniel got up to walk again. As they walked through the park on the cobblestoned path, Daniel noticed kids playing with their parents, and tons of people running or bicycling through the park. After a short walk, they came upon a football field. John asked, "You know who Vince Lombardi was?"

"Absolutely! I'm a huge Green Bay Packers fan."

"One of the most famous talks he ever gave to his team—mind you, this was a group of professional male athletes—started by asking, 'What is the meaning of love?' And he went on to say: 'Anybody can love something that is beautiful or smart or agile. You will never know love until you can love something that isn't beautiful, isn't bright, isn't glamorous. It takes a special person to love something unattractive, someone unknown. That is the test of love. Everybody can love someone's strengths and good looks. But can you accept someone for his inabilities?' The truth is, Daniel, I want to help you develop and improve on your leadership tactics as a coach, but if you don't change the way you see people, you will just be using them to fulfill your own needs. People fail as leaders—even with all the tricks from leadership books—because the people they lead can see past their motivational tricks. They can sense and feel a leader's heart posture. If you don't prove to them you care for them as people first, you'll never get anywhere in your profession. You can compliment them or feed them lines all day long, but people have a way of sensing if you are real or not. It's up to you to find that internal love and project it to the external world. No one can do it but you. And if you choose not to, then good luck trying to get these kids to get you a bottle of water, nonetheless play their hearts out for you."

Daniel's shoulders drooped, knowing John was spot on with his remarks. "I can get so focused on treating people the way I think they deserve to be treated, instead of doing what I know great leaders do: treat people *better* than they think they deserve to be treated. That's a huge problem for me. I'm sure they see through my BS."

As John and Daniel headed back to the car, John reminded him, "If we withdraw our love based on what they do, that is transactional leadership. We need them to know they are loved, not just hear it. Love them for who they are, not what they do."

Daniel excitedly replied, "I gotta shift my attitude here. It obviously affects the way I'm doing things, and the way I'm doing things just isn't working for my team or me. So if I don't change my beliefs, my actions won't change either. But how do I retrain my attitude? I can't help but get so frustrated by the things they do! And I have been thinking this way for the better part of my life. It isn't like a light switch I can just flip on and off."

"Great question, Daniel. Acknowledge your thoughts, but don't accept them. Every day, for the next thirty days, write down the name of everyone on your team and write something new and positive about that person. Don't let yourself slip into the negative here. You've already written down every name, and you seemed to choose a negative adjective for each one. The question I'd leave you with is: Does that reflect who they are or how you feel about them?"

As Daniel pondered the question his shoulders sagged as he realized he was being far too critical of the young men he was leading.

CHAPTER 17

MODEL THE GREAT COACHES

Daniel had three weeks to make the necessary efforts to turn things around this summer. He had a million things he wanted to accomplish, and the clock was ticking. Daniel felt inspired to try new things out with his team, but he also recognized a great deal of focus would need to be on himself—the example he set for those around him, and the way he operated and responded to difficult situations as they might arise. He was going to have to reinvent himself, one step at a time. This wouldn't be an easy task, but Daniel felt recharged and motivated to give it every ounce of effort he had available to him. He would go down swinging.

After reading about so many of the great musicians, artists, writers, and even athletes this world has come to know, he realized they all copied their heroes that came before them. The Beatles had spent years copying Buddy Holly, Little Richard, Jerry Lee Lewis, and Elvis Presley. The great composer Mozart spent the first decade of his career copying his favorite works. Even Kobe Bryant admitted to studying his favorite players—especially Michael Jordan—to learn how to play the game. That inspired Daniel to dig deep into his past and think about those coaches he respected the most. One stood out above the rest.

Daniel had decided to start by copying his hero, the legendary San Antonio Spurs coach Gregg Popovich. In an effort to really understand why Popovich did what he did, Daniel had spent the last month studying him. He read and watched everything he could find on "Pop," as his players referred to him. By imitating the behaviors, tactics, and style of great coaches like Gregg Popovich, Anson Dorrance, and John Wooden, he would be able to develop a new coaching style that fit his personality while giving a nod to the strategies and behaviors that helped these coaches reach massive levels of success with their players.

One of the most powerful stories Daniel read about Gregg Popovich referenced the first thing "Pop" did after they drafted future NBA MVP and Hall of Famer Tim Duncan. "Pop" decided to take a vacation with Duncan to his hometown of St. Croix. They ate, drank, relaxed, and swam together, and he got to know Tim Duncan as a person before he took the first step in the gym with him. Popovich valued relationships first, so that was where Daniel would start. Daniel's number-one value was love, and his mission already included helping young men lead with love. It was time to practice what he preached.

> **Reflect and write: Who are some of your heroes or biggest role models? How might you imitate them?**

Daniel stopped by John's house for a quick chat. "Well, John, we're only a couple days away from our first summer practice. I'm a little worried."

"Then let's build an action plan. What's your number-one focus for the next three weeks?"

"Becoming an example to my team that is really worth following."

"And what's the first step?"

"Love. I need to build loving relationships."

"Great. Now, in all your notes from the things you have read, our conversations, and your experiences, what can you commit to doing the first week before the season starts? Remember, it needs to be something really small that you can absolutely accomplish without issue. Things you can do in just a couple minutes, and they have to align with your principles and goals for the week. They need to be intentional and measurable."

Daniel smiled, excited to start bringing things together. "Gotcha, John. Just like Mother Teresa said, 'Be faithful in the small things, for it is in them that your strength lies.'"

John nodded. "Very good! Now, start small; just do one small thing the first day, then the second day add another, and then another. You get the idea."

Daniel got up, shook John's hand, and hurried out the door. He was ready to get down to business and see if he could channel his inner "Pop."

———

For Daniel, it was an invigorating first week of summer practice. It brought him back to the beginning of his career, and he felt those same butterflies he had in the first few practices as a head coach. After fifteen years of coaching, he felt uncomfortable and unsure of himself again, but he could sense some progress in the relationships and a more positive culture forming within the team.

He stayed consistent in his personal training by writing something positive in his journal about each player the night before. This was an effort to see the young men on his team as people, not just athletes. Before the first practice, he moved around the gym instead of standing huddled with his coaches. He was high-fiving and even sometimes hugging guys as they came in. He would ask about their day, their family, or if they watched the big NBA game last night.

As the practices progressed, Daniel found new small ways to be vulnerable each day. His first decision was to thank all the players for allowing him to coach them and supporting him as he tried to grow as a leader. Sometimes, he admitted he was unsure of the best defensive strategy for the team and asked for their opinions. Instead of teasing the guys, he made fun of himself for being old, boring, and out of touch. After the team failed miserably to run a relatively simple drill, Daniel responded by taking responsibility and acknowledging that he did a poor job explaining and teaching it to them. He remembered that meaningful connections come by acknowledging your feelings, challenges, and shortcomings.

By the middle of the week, Daniel focused on his proximity, body language, and spacing when speaking with guys on a one-on-one basis. Daniel tried to get closer to each player, make eye contact, and speak warmly to them. He knew that doing so would help build relationships.

He spent time at the end of every practice meeting with a few players one-on-one to ask them the following three questions:

1. What do you like most about our program?
2. What do you like least about our program?
3. What would you change if you were the coach?

Answers varied from the things they did in practice, the offenses they ran, the teams they played, and the tournaments they entered. Archie, who still had his walls up even after Daniel had apologized a month earlier, seemed to be the most honest with him. He indicated he'd yell less if he were the coach. It was hard for Daniel to hear that type of feedback and left him feeling inclined to justify his actions. However, he knew that great leaders embrace the hard criticism, regardless of how they feel.

As Daniel wrapped the first couple weeks of practice, he felt as if he had done a pretty good job of modeling his coaching heroes. He knew it would feel more like a marathon than a short sprint, but that didn't deter him from putting his head down and remaining dedicated to progress and building strong relationships with his team. But even then, Daniel knew it would be no easy feat to get these kids to buy in and play their hearts out.

CHAPTER 18

ADVOCACY BEFORE ACCOUNTABILITY

As positive as the week had gone for Daniel, he was tired of the lack of discipline and the players taking advantage of his kindness. He met with John for coffee on Saturday morning. He walked into the diner, and noticed John sitting next to a tall, lanky, curly-haired man.

"Daniel, this is Willy, one of my former players. He's going to join us today."

Daniel was excited and couldn't wait to hear some stories about John from one of his players. "Great to meet you, Willy," Daniel said as he shook his hand.

Willy's face bubbled with joy. "The pleasure is mine! Coach has told me a great deal about you!"

After they all finished eating and talking about family and their lives outside of basketball, John asked Daniel, "So, tell me, what went well this week?"

"Well, I feel like the relationships have grown, and I laid down a solid foundation with most of my players. I'm definitely starting to see them more as people, rather than objects or obstacles, but I'm still really struggling to look past the lack of effort and complacency. All this vulnerability and love is great, but what about discipline, accountability, high standards, and expectations? I know you can't have a great culture without those!"

John paused, as if to consider the comments. He slowly responded, "Those will come with time. People are often too eager to impose their vision on their team and become the accountability police. A friend of mine named Jack Easterby once told me, accountability is just accounting for someone's ability. As leaders, we need to identify the struggles of each individual person within our program, and then walk with them on their journey. Remember this: advocacy before accountability. It's a key principle to calling up. Advocacy is about serving each individual and supporting their agenda. How can you be their advocate?"

Daniel replied with a sense of confidence he hadn't quite had before. "By having great conversations that connect with the person, not the player. And those conversations start with great questions, and understanding their agenda, their purpose, and what they struggle with. Without these, they're like ships setting sail on the ocean with no map, compass, or direction."

"Exactly! With a meaningful relationship and shared vision, now you can address some of the behavior issues." John nodded. "Now share with me, what are the biggest challenges?"

"Kids are showing up late, some of the guys aren't really competing, and I constantly have to ask them to listen when their teammates and I are talking. I really feel like I need to talk to them about the importance of doing those things, or else I'll be condoning it."

John smiled. "*Condoning* it . . . that's a great point. You get what you tolerate, absolutely. But talking at them is not the solution. I learned long ago that lectures don't have half the effect of consequences."

"So, I need to start enforcing some rules, right? I mean, if they're not punished for showing up late, they will continue to show up late."

"Daniel, I want you to look at this through a new lens. Adults love to create rules, but those are all about calling people out. Call people up by creating some boundaries. Start with your non-negotiables and communicate them not as rules and punishment, but as boundaries and consequences. Punishment is about the past. It is something you do to others. Consequences are about the future; they're something they do to themselves. Be sure to start by discussing the positive consequences of living in the boundaries. Some people struggle to see the difference but being intentional about what you call it will help players see it as something they did to themselves, rather than something you did to them."

Daniel got out his notebook and wrote down the differences. "I think I get it. Rules and punishment are how coaches lead with fear. Boundaries and consequences offer players freedom through structure."

"Precisely! Discipline is about teaching, not punishing. We need to give them the autonomy to make choices and suffer consequences, rather than trying to control them through fear. In today's society, adults often try to intervene because they love their child. But love needs truth, and without boundaries, we let their problems become ours and end up raising children, not adults."

"I understand the difference, but how do I apply consequences without them being a rule or punishment?" Daniel asked.

"Well, when I started out in coaching, I had a lot of boundaries and few suggestions. That changed later on in coaching. I had fewer boundaries and more suggestions. So, start simple! As you start your actual season, you will empower players to create more boundaries for themselves and each other, but for now, what are your non-negotiables? What will provide a foundation to enable you to do your job as the leader of the team? For me, I only had three non-negotiables. What are yours?"

Daniel took the time to think about what really mattered. What did he need as a foundation to move forward? What really mattered to him? He really valued time, he always wanted players competing in games or drills to be at their best, and he believed it was the most disrespectful thing not to listen when someone else spoke.

"Okay," he said. "I'll start with three:

1. Be on time
2. Always compete
3. Listen to the person who is talking."

Reflect and write: What are your non-negotiables?

Willy, who had been fairly quiet until now, chimed in. "Great non-negotiables are simple, clear, and important, and they apply to everyone. Coach always did a great job communicating boundaries and consequences in a way that let us know they were for our own personal good and the success of the team! They weren't about him or holding some power over us."

John nodded. "I always tried to communicate the benefit of doing certain things and the consequence of failing to do certain things. You want them to see how actions lead to outcomes. During the course of the season and practices, remind them of this by encouraging them to meet expectations because it will help them get where they want to go."

Daniel nodded. "So what do I do when they don't live within the boundaries?"

"It'll be easy to want to hold them accountable, but remember, you've first got to be an advocate! Help them self-evaluate. If they're not competing, ask them to rate their competitiveness on a scale of one to five. Usually, they will be honest. Then ask, 'What can you do right now to start being more competitive?' When they fail to show up on time, ask, 'What can you do to make sure you make it on time in the future?' When they fail to listen or respect a coach or teammate who is talking, ask, 'What can you do to help yourself focus when someone else is speaking?' Remember: advocacy before accountability!"

Daniel jotted down notes. He knew this was going to be critical, and the little details and language were absolutely important to ensure that he did it the right way. Then he asked, "So the majority will follow if I create and communicate my non-negotiables. I can redirect those who don't by making little nudges or adjustments and helping them self-evaluate. But what about the individuals who still fail to meet expectations? Do I make them run or do other conditioning? Or do I just try to reward those who meet the expectations?"

"Carrots can be effective. Sticks can be effective. But are we looking for obedience and compliance or to develop the character to manage their emotions, empathize with others, and persevere through setbacks? Are we trying to build virtue? They should want to be at practice on time, listening and competing because of the positive consequences. If they fail to meet expectations, they shouldn't have the privilege of practicing or playing that day."

"So I just tell them they can't practice? They're being lazy to begin with! They will love that! And what about on a game day? Sitting your best player isn't easy!"

Willy chuckled. "Oh boy, do I remember a few times Coach enforced the boundaries with me. I was an All-American going into my second season with Coach, and I thought I could show up to practice with a beard and long hair. Didn't match Coach's definition of neat and clean. I told him I thought it was my right to grow a beard and have my hair as long as I wanted. You know what he said to me? 'I respect your right, Willy, and I'm disappointed that you won't be playing for us this season.' Well, I sprinted to the training room, cut my hair right there, borrowed a razor, and shaved as quickly as I could, and still made it to practice in time."

Daniel laughed. "Are you serious? That's incredible."

"He would leave players behind that didn't show up on time to the bus. I wasn't so lucky another time; I tried to get away without shaving for half a week. When I got to the bus two minutes before it was supposed to leave for a game against our cross-town rivals, Coach saw me trotting in and let me know that I couldn't play. I told him I would go shave, and he just wished me luck in finding transportation to the game! It was amazing; he never got angry or yelled."

John smiled. "I might have seemed cool and collected, but inside, I was a little worried about not having my best player for one of our strongest opponents. Still, I knew it was important to the culture of the team, my relationship with my players, and the personal development of each person. You have to be honest and truthful; love doesn't exist without it. I let them know the truth, while also reminding them of their value in an effort to keep it positive."

Daniel thought about all the times he had yelled at his players. "I get so angry because I take things personally. I remember seeing a sign once that said, 'People don't do things because of us; they do things because of who they are.' That's important to remember when it comes to enforcing the boundaries out of love. To call them up, I have to lead them to a place where they can see what they did and how it negatively affects the people around them. But what happens if all of this doesn't work?"

John grew sad as he answered Daniel. "It was once said, 'The wise learn by instruction, the slow learn by correction, the foolish learn by consequences, and the selfish never learn.' At some stage, we have to let our team and players suffer the natural consequences. It may be an experience of losing because they're out of shape or unprepared. Those can be powerful teaching moments. Other times, the consequences may have to be even more severe. Those unwilling to accept the non-negotiables . . . well, they should be encouraged to look for a new team. Those are the consequences that can often be very painful."

Daniel nodded. "We have four practices left before we go to our summer team camp, and I know I have some work to do to help them see practice and team camp as a privilege, not an entitlement."

John smiled. "You're absolutely right. Adults today complain a lot about an entitled generation. Kids are not born more entitled, it's the way we're raising them. I know you're going to keep thinking about the way you discipline your team so that you can nurture the relationship with your players."

CHAPTER 19

A NEW MODE OF OPERATING

Daniel felt inspired after his most recent conversation with John. But that quickly subsided, as a quarter of the team showed up late on Monday. However, today Daniel felt more equipped to use these moments as opportunities for growth, rather than to wallow in self-pity or take it out on his team. He had really worked hard to retrain the way he operated in these challenging moments, and this was an opportunity to show off his new style.

Instead of punishing players in an effort to get obedience and compliance, Daniel would work to enforce the boundaries with the person in mind, disciplining in a way that would develop the character essential to overcome challenges, criticism, and frustrations. In these moments of conflict, the players would develop the self-control to hold themselves and each other accountable, without a coach looming over them. He would be disciplining to teach, not punish. As Daniel got the team to huddle together, he pushed through his fear and spoke clearly, concisely, and calmly in laying out the non-negotiables.

"Fellas. We are in our second and last week of summer practice before we head to team camp. In order for us to move forward as a team and continue growing, there are some things we are *all* going to need to start doing consistently. One: be on time. Two: compete. Compete in every drill or game to be at *your* best. And three: when a coach or player is talking, we are to listen with eyes and ears. Practices will be more beneficial and enjoyable if we do these three things. We will maximize our potential, prepare ourselves for the weekend games, and build a better team culture. If we fail to do these three things . . . well, you are going to lose the opportunity—the privilege—to practice or play in games this weekend at camp." Daniel paused for fifteen seconds to let it soak in. "Any questions?"

Aaron spoke up. "What if our car breaks down or our parents don't get us to practice on time?"

Daniel smiled and nodded. "Great question, Aaron; we need people to ask more good questions like that one. Communicate. If you're going to be late, then it is on you to call and let me know. I will do my best to be fair."

Eddie then asked, "What if we're hurt and having a hard time playing ball?"

"Good point, Eddie. Communicate injuries. Communicate when things off the court are really making it challenging to compete at your best."

Daniel looked around and spotted many of the players that showed up late. "We had quite a large number of people who showed up late today. Starting tomorrow, if you choose to be late, you will lose the opportunity to come in and get better. What can you do to ensure you get out of bed and get to practice on time?"

The players suggested different ideas, from setting multiple alarms and texting each other, to leaving fifteen minutes early.

"Great suggestions. Let's make it happen; I know you can."

There was an air of positive energy during practice, and the young men worked hard—except for Aaron and Archie. Daniel pulled Archie aside.

"Anything I should know about?"

"No, why?"

"Well, on a scale of one to five, how hard are you competing?"

"Umm. Probably a two. "

"What can you do to pick it up?"

"I don't know. I guess I could start sprinting up the court and getting into a defensive stance."

"Fantastic!"

Only a few minutes later, it was Aaron who let his man go right past him for the third time. Daniel called him over. He walked right up to Daniel, head down, avoiding his gaze.

"Aaron, anything I need to know?"

"No," he said, clearly irritated.

"How hard are you competing, on a scale from one to five?"

"I don't know. I don't like this drill. When can we scrimmage?"

"Aaron, we know you're not giving even close to your best; the team needs you to pick it up, as it's not helping you or anybody else when you give that type of effort. What can you do to pick it up?"

"I don't know. I guess play defense."

"What will you do if you're playing harder on defense?"

"Uhh . . . move my feet."

"Great! You're the fastest guy on the team; I know people aren't going to get by you when you start competing at your best. It just won't happen."

Archie picked up the effort almost immediately. It wasn't perfect, but it was progress, and that was what Daniel was looking for. Aaron, on the other hand, continued to dog it through drills, allowing much slower players to beat him. A few minutes later, Daniel was speaking to him again. "Aaron, if you don't start competing, you're going to lose the privilege to practice today."

Aaron brushed Daniel off and actually gave even less effort. Daniel was furious. How could he do this to him? He then remembered that it wasn't about himself, it was about Aaron. He spoke directly to his young player.

"Aaron—please put your practice uniform in the wash and head home for the day. You have lost the opportunity to get better. We hope to see you tomorrow, on time, and ready to compete."

Aaron's face turned from apathy to rage. "Who do you think you are, kicking me out of practice? The drill is stupid, and I'm better than any player here. Forget about this team, man! Forget about you!" And with that, he stormed out of the gym.

Aaron skipped the next practice but showed up later in the week. Although he was on time and competed hard, because he had missed two of the last three practices and didn't meet team expectations, Daniel chose not to allow him to play at the team camp that weekend.

At the second practice of the week, only two players showed up late. They weren't allowed to practice, and that sent a message to the rest of the team. Everyone else was on time. Both of the late players voluntarily apologized to Daniel and the team. While Daniel still had to correct and help players self-evaluate their lack of competitiveness or inattention, he didn't have to ask anybody else to leave practice. His message was clear— he would not tolerate people showing up late, failing to compete, and not listening in practice.

Outside of his non-negotiables, there were a lot of other little things that Daniel knew they needed to do a better job of that gave him concerns. But he trusted John's guidance and just offered "suggestions" instead of trying to impose more rules. So Daniel focused on some of the intangibles: no foul language, cleaning up after themselves, working hard, and all the other little positive habits he hoped to build. He shifted to working on the positive instead of just ordering the kids around, and constantly reminded them to act in accordance with who they wanted to become.

Daniel spent the second week of the team camp continuing to nurture the relationships with his players by staying committed to the behaviors he outlined in the first week. He noticed some significant progress among much of his team at the end of the first two weeks, but some of the players still remained stagnant. He returned home after camp and went for a walk with John to recount the last few days with his team and share his concerns for the future.

John affirmed Daniel's concerns. "You still have great challenges ahead of you, but it's great that you continue to see everything that happens as an opportunity to learn and grow. Trust the process. You have started to retrain your *default mode of operation*, but that is a never-ending process. Continue to refine that process by adding and doing little things every day to grow personally. So when you face the big, challenging decisions, you will be prepared to act as a man of principle, not as a man ruled by emotion."

"What are the things you did every day that helped you grow?" Daniel asked.

"It was not an overnight process, but an *overtime process* where I developed some essential habits that worked for me. If I were going to be at my best, I needed to eat right, exercise for at least twenty minutes, and get seven hours of sleep each night! Too many coaches act tough by working all night long, eating junk food, and letting themselves go. Not only does it hold them back from being their best selves, but it sets a poor example for the people on their team. My other essential habits included a daily routine of prayer, reading, and journaling. Prayer strengthens my spirit. Reading strengthens me intellectually. And journaling strengthens me mentally. The benefits are immense, and some days it would be just for a few minutes in the morning."

> **Reflect and write: What are some daily disciplines that align with your coaching manifesto (philosophy)? What small daily habits are you committed to developing for you to be the best coach you can be?**

Daniel was amazed. "You still do all of that today?"

"Yup. Even as an old dog, I'm still learning and growing."

Daniel hugged John before dropping him off at home. "Thank you. Without your guidance and support these last few months, I'm not sure I would have made it through these challenges. These kids can really put you to task. But I'm seeing some changes, and the small glimpses are really inspiring. They keep me going and focused to keep moving forward. Even though I know Brownie loves me and supports me, I can feel so alone and under attack by all the unhappy parents and disgruntled players. It's great to have you believe in me and to talk with someone who has gone through so many of the same challenges."

John put his hand on Daniel's shoulder, smiled at him, and said, "Daniel—the hard work is on your shoulders. I do what I can to guide you and walk with you on this journey. But in the end, I'm not sitting in your practices or facing these challenges myself. It is on you. Only you can do better, handle these challenges, and teach these young men to become responsible adults. It will happen, I'm confident of it. But only if you stay the course, weather the storm, and remain calm even when they push you to the edge. This is your new modus operandi."

PART III
BUILDING THE TEAM

Tremendous leaders call up others! They help them rise to greatness and create a system that promotes the greater good of the team. Your finish line might seem galaxies away, but just like your personal journey, your team's journey starts small and gets bigger and bigger as you inch closer to your goals. If this journey were easy, or if we saw the progress quickly, then more people would take this path. In fact, we'd all likely be great leaders. But that is certainly not the case. It takes grit, persistence, and an effort like no other.

Part III of our story focuses on how Daniel intentionally lays the foundation for his team, puts them through a grueling training camp meant to test their character as much as their skillset, and then selects the right players, not the most talented ones. It would be impractical and nearly impossible to do everything that Daniel does in a *lifetime* of coaching, much less one year. The purpose of the story is to expand upon the principles and show how other coaches have put them into action.

CHAPTER 20

BUILD YOUR CIRCLE

The off-season break began shortly after the first two weeks of summer practice. Daniel felt there were a great deal of highs and lows, but overall he knew there was progress within his team. Still, Daniel faced another uphill battle with his team. While he had made progress on the complicated situation with his players, he still had to focus on developing his coaching staff.

Of the four coaches on staff, two had left and two had remained. That left Daniel with a sense of unease. He understood it was essential to develop a staff aligned with his vision for the direction of the program if he were to have any chance of success. But how would he get them to buy in? He faced several challenges in doing so, so he met John one sunny autumn Sunday to discuss his next best steps.

John asked Daniel to take him to a place they had never visited together—a cemetery. John wanted to place flowers on his wife's grave. They arrived at the cemetery, and John weaved in and out of the gravestones, eventually making it to one with the name of his wife on it. It was an impeccably kept quaint gravestone. It was clear to Daniel that John regularly visited his wife and ensured her marking was well tended to. Daniel watched as John got on his knees, placed flowers on the grave, and left a stack of letters behind. John slowly stood up and walked with Daniel along a path through the cemetery. Daniel wanted to be respectful but couldn't help asking what he thought was an obvious question. "Why did you leave a stack of letters on the grave?"

John looked up with tears in his eyes. "Old habits die hard. Years ago, I started to write my wife a love note every day. I thought it would be an essential habit for a great marriage. As I did it over the years, I realized more and more that writing those notes was just as good for me as it was for her. I kept writing those notes even after she passed away nearly twenty years ago. And I would deliver them to her every Sunday afternoon with some flowers, rain or shine." As he recounted his story, it was clear he loved his wife now just as much as he had on the last day she spent on earth. This blew Daniel away.

As they walked along, John's attention turned to Daniel. "You mentioned you have some big challenges ahead with your coaching staff. What opportunities are you seeing here?"

Daniel smiled. With a hint of sarcasm, he said, "Ah yes, my challenges are just opportunities. Well, I need to hire two more coaches, and it's not easy to find people willing to commit to the program, because we have such a small budget!"

"Well, I think in most lines of work, regardless of money, leaders struggle to find the right people, but it's often because we are offering the wrong things! Remember, people want to be a part of something greater than themselves. Rather than looking to entice people with a measly stipend or a coaching title, offer them the opportunity to be transformed and to transform others!" As John said this, he veered off the path through a group of old graves.

Daniel nodded and replied, "Great point! Building a coaching staff should look a lot like building your team of players. I guess it really is all part of the same thing."

John stopped in front of one very old grave. It was very large—easily ten times larger than every grave around it, and it had probably cost tens of thousands of dollars. At the top was the name *Andrew Carnegie*.

Daniel read the engraving across the bottom of the tombstone. "Here lies a man who was wise enough to bring into his service men who knew more than he."

"Daniel, find a small group of people who trust the process, who believe in you, and who are committed to the mission. Wise leaders look to bring in people with strengths in areas where they are weak and then give them the freedom to lead. They don't get in the way of progress, but rather empower the team to do amazing things. *Leaders create more leaders.* Oh, and one more thing—great leaders look for 'yes men' who will say no. These are people who are strong enough to share their opinions and disagree, but when it is time to move forward, they are able to commit, buy in, and follow the plan outlined to them. Those are the best types of coaches, as they will respect your leadership but never allow you to settle for less than your best."

Daniel nodded. "That makes sense. Up until this point, I had a transactional approach to my coaches—looking to get more out of them, instead of giving more to them. I think we need to bond and figure out how to work together as one. You know what? I think I'll start by taking them on a special retreat to a very special mountain!"

After hiring two new young assistants, Daniel found a warm weekend in early September to hike Clearview Mountain with them. Luckily, the weather looked great and hiking would be a great deal easier this time around, as there were no storms or snow in the forecast. A month before the retreat, he gave his coaching staff a book for them to read and a walking program to help them build the strength necessary to hike the mountain.

Fred, Chad, Mark, and Taylor were all on his newly assembled staff. Fred was the older assistant and a typical old-school kind of guy. He seemed to be genuinely excited at the prospect of getting outside to enjoy the outdoors for a few days. Chad was a young guy returning from the previous season. He had been unsure of himself last year, and Daniel knew he had to give him more opportunities to lead. Mark was a new assistant—middle-aged, with a great deal of experience, and he seemed to be really passionate about his job. Taylor was also a new assistant—very young, loved the game, but didn't seem to possess much leadership experience or any coaching experience. It was really a mixed bag of tricks, but Daniel knew he'd have to find a way to bring everyone together in a synergistic way if they ever hoped to reach their goals.

Of course, the first thing Daniel did was contact his old buddy James to ask him if he'd be interested in leading his coaches on a journey up the mountain. Daniel was excited to start the journey that James was leading. Hopefully it would be two days up and one day down, but Daniel was okay with the possibility that they might not make it to the peak. He knew it was about the experience. He just hoped he could persuade his fellow coaches of the same thing.

Daniel spent the first day on the mountain asking his coaches questions to get to know them better as people. Even though he had known Fred and Chad for a few years, he had never asked them much about their lives, pasts, or families. To break the ice, Daniel decided to open up about some of his own life. He hoped his coaches would then reciprocate. As they chatted with one another, James led them up the mountain. At different breaking points, James would stop and share stories and experiences with the group, same as he did when Daniel had first climbed the mountain.

They gathered around the fire later that evening. Daniel was nervous, scared, and felt a weight on his shoulders. "Well, before I ask you all what you thought of the book, I feel like I need to share something with you all. I don't normally talk like this, but I think it's important for you to know how I feel about the forthcoming season. I'm scared because my job is on the line. It's hard to admit that, but it's the truth, and you all need to know it. Still, I made the trip up this mountain some months ago, and when I did, I started to see things in a new light. Instead of just surviving, winning some games, and keeping my job this season, I want a totally different experience. I want to use our platform to help transform the lives of the young men we have the opportunity to lead. Doing that is not easy, and it really has started with me working daily to retrain my thinking and my default mode of operation." Daniel looked around the group. "I'm asking you all not to just work with me to create a transformational culture for our players, but to work with me to become a better coach and person. I need to be able to count on your support, but also your honest feedback at times. It will not be easy for me to hear all the time, but I will appreciate and embrace it, because there is so much I can and need to do to get better this year. And it starts with listening to you and empowering you."

The coaches—who, up until now, had been a little anxious—relaxed a little as Daniel addressed the elephant in the room: that he might lose his job at the end of the year. While Mark still seemed a little withdrawn, Fred, Chad, and Taylor all chimed in with their support and appreciation for Daniel's decision to share with them and bring them in on this experience. Over the next four hours, they discussed the book they had read during the off-season, and Daniel listened intently, instead of trying to be the smartest guy in the room or the authority figure. He was more focused on listening and learning from his staff.

Daniel then shifted to questions beyond the book. He looked for feedback on previous seasons, issues they noticed, and positives they saw. He had his journal out and was rapidly taking notes. Every time someone challenged the way he had been doing things, he embraced the criticism by saying things like, "Fantastic, I need more ideas like that!"

Daniel felt closer to his coaches by the end of the evening. Some things had been uncomfortable to hear, but he was at least glad to know what they were thinking, even if he didn't agree with everything they said. At times, it was hard not to respond and defend his thinking, but he was more interested in solutions, not excuses.

As they climbed the final stages of the mountain the next day, the coaches were buzzing with energy. It seemed like in just one night they had transformed from a staff to a team, and definitely felt more connected. They laughed and shared funny stories of previous seasons. Daniel even made fun of himself and the crazy things he had done as a coach, something he never would have done before.

When they reached the top of the mountain, Daniel pulled out a copy of his coaching manifesto and shared it with all of them. After sharing, he said, "Joe Ehrmann suggests that every coaching staff should have a coaching contract. Well, I would like to suggest that we all create a very simple coaching staff manifesto. We need to answer these important questions: What is our purpose? Our core values? What are we committed to doing? How will we operate? What are the roles each of us can play to best serve the team? We all have strengths, so let's make sure we are maximizing them! Lastly, how will we define and measure success as a coaching staff?"

Reflect and write: What challenges do you face with a coaching staff or lack of coaching staff? How might you see these as opportunities?

Starting with the questions Daniel had used to create his own manifesto, the staff then came up with a very simple and straightforward staff manifesto. Lastly, they worked to define success as a staff. Success would be realized when every member of the team knew three things: that they are special, they are loved, and their value comes from who they were as people not from what they do on the court. As well as this activity went, Mark had not shared nearly as much as the others and seemed distant. All day and the night before, he had looked for opportunities to talk about tactics and skill development. Daniel knew he had to address the issue to see how he could help.

As Mark sat looking out over Clearview Mountain, Daniel approached him and asked, "What's on your mind?"

Mark looked back at him, clearly hesitating to respond. Daniel pushed on. "Seriously, share with me, whatever it is."

Mark took a deep breath. "All this talk about character, purpose, and commitments—it sounds great and all, but I'm ready to talk about basketball. We won't win any games if we don't have any talent and can't execute on both sides of the ball."

"I appreciate your concerns, Mark. Trust me when I say I'm excited to talk about the x's and o's, but we need to take care of other things first. Building a winning team will mean nothing to us if we don't first build a transformational culture. Then, we can talk about basketball all you want. I can promise you that."

A scowl came across Mark's face. "Well, you won't be leading anybody if you aren't winning. You'll be out of a job, and I will have wasted a year of my life. You're a sinking ship! I need you to know that I want to go somewhere in coaching and accomplish big things. I don't want to be an assistant coach all my life. I'd hate for you to screw this up for me because you're worried about the touchy-feely stuff and not about winning!"

Daniel felt as if he had been punched in the face. While he wanted to snap, he took a deep breath before calmly responding, "Well, I really believe that if we take care of our culture first, the rest will only be enhanced. I can't control whether they fire me or not, but I can control how I lead. I hope you can come on board, because we could really use a coach with your level of training and tactical experience. I'm happy to meet with you regularly to help you on that journey, but by the time the season starts, I'll need you to be all in. Otherwise, you'll need to find another team to coach for."

Daniel offered Mark his hand, and he grudgingly but firmly shook it. He patted his disgruntled coach on the back, wondering if Mark was going to be the type of coach he wanted on his team. Either way, Daniel knew he would do the best he could to lead and hoped Mark was willing to buy into the process.

The remainder of the journey down the mountain was a peaceful one. The staff enjoyed talking more about their families, upbringing, and their respective roads to coaching. It was important that they bonded on this trip, because they were about to face the most difficult season of their careers.

CHAPTER 21

VALUE YOUR VALUES

Daniel felt invigorated after returning home from Clearview Mountain. While his second visit was much less challenging than his first, it was every bit as inspiring and motivating. He just hoped his coaches felt the same way. Daniel sat with his assistants the following weekend, watching a middle school AAU tournament that Washington Prep hosted. One eighth-grade team was demolishing the other, which wasn't unusual in travel tournaments. What *was* unusual was an eighth-grader named Jaylen, who had just racked up his tenth dunk of the game. The fans were buzzing with excitement and admiration. They cheered every time he got the ball, knowing it was quite likely he'd do something special to entertain the packed audience.

Daniel leaned back in his seat and said to his staff, "Jaylen sure reminds me a lot of Jayden. And it's not just the name."

He saw Mark's eyes sparkle as Jaylen threw down another violent dunk. "This kid is unbelievable! The team that gets him is going to spend the next four years dominating this area." As soon as he finished the statement, Daniel watched Jaylen cockily look at the crowd and throw his hands in the air while raising the roof.

Bill, the Washington Prep athletic director, joined the coaches in the bleachers. "The player seeking the clap on the back is like a gladiator, he will only survive as long as he wins."[8]

---

8   *Less than a Minute to Go* by Bill Thierfelder

133

"Absolutely!" Fred chimed in. "Just wait until things don't go his way; then he'll struggle. Just like Daniel said—this guy is way too similar to Jayden. We don't need another Jayden on our team. One bad attitude is enough for me."

Taylor leaned forward in his chair. "But he has so much potential! I've been reading Carol Dweck's book *Mindset*, and she says that we can cultivate our basic qualities and character through hard work, just like any other skill. He would need some work, but isn't that a coach's responsibility?"

Daniel chuckled and shook his head. "Building a high-performance culture starts with character. The All Blacks rugby team—the highest achieving sports team of the last century have a saying, 'Great people make great All Blacks.' Jaylen has ability, but what he chooses to do with it might be an entirely different story. Ever see the film *Moneyball* about Billy Beane? He was supposed to be the greatest player ever, but instead was the greatest bust ever. Ability, especially at a young age, can be a distraction from something just as important—mindset."

Irritated, Mark abruptly spoke up. "Show me a team that can win without talent."

"I think we have to start walking the walk," Chad said. "If you say you value hardworking, resilient, and grateful individuals, those have got to be the people you bring into the program. We can't fall victim to the naturalness bias."

> **Reflect and write: How have you selected players in the past? Are your values reflected in the players you choose?**

"What's the naturalness bias?" Taylor asked.

"Prejudice against people who have achieved by working for it and preference for those who appear to have achieved with natural talent or gifts," Chad responded. "Essentially, people think they value effort, but they don't. They value and admire what is easy or comes naturally."

Suddenly, Jaylen was driving to the basket when a tall, lanky white kid named Steve jumped out of nowhere to block his shot. Jaylen looked at the referee for a foul, leaving Steve to dribble down the court for an uncontested lay-up. For the next three plays, Jaylen forced up shots, complained to the referee, and all the while, Steve grabbed rebounds, passed to his teammates, and hustled up and down the floor. Jaylen's coach called a time-out, and not surprisingly Jaylen sulked over to the bench.

Daniel frowned and looked to the coaches and then to Bill. "He doesn't know how to fail. And that's why Billy Beane failed. Unless Jaylen can learn how to fail, his story will be just like Billy's."

"I've been an athletic director for a long time now," Bill interjected, "and I'll tell you this: the best coaches aren't the ones with the most ability. Ability is common enough. The critical measure of great coaches is the ability to create an environment that develops the ability *and* mindset of others."

"Exactly," Fred said. "We need to find young people who love to learn and improve, not just win."

"So, you're saying we are just going to forget about a player's ability altogether?" Mark exclaimed.

As the game ended, the coaches watched Jaylen walk through the high-five line with the other team, ignoring every person he walked past because he looked into the crowd so intently. On the other side, the coaches observed Steve comfort a teammate by putting his arm around him as they walked to the locker room.

Shaking his head, Daniel looked Mark directly in the eyes. "We shouldn't be looking for the best player, just the right players. I know we can't ignore a player's ability. But we can't keep ignoring attitude and effort. I might have the fastest car on the block, but I'm not going anywhere without any gas. Character is our fuel; without it, we go nowhere."

With only a month left until tryouts began, Daniel went home to write a letter to the team, letting them know the start date and time of the tryouts. He knew it was important to communicate his core values to the team before they stepped foot in the gym. He started the letter by being vulnerable, clearly communicating his expectations, core values, and non-negotiables. He was calling them up to join him on a transformational journey.

To All Prospective Washington Prep Basketball Players,

Some of you have played for me in previous seasons. For others, this will be your first time. Regardless of my past failings and short-comings, I hope you will all give me a clean slate this season. Over the course of the off-season, I have strived to become a better coach, leader, and person, and I will continue on that journey when the season begins. I hope you will all join me in growing as men. In the past, tryouts have selected players largely based on a player's ability, but I want to be upfront and clear that things will change.

First, my mission this season is to help you grow into virtuous men who will lead with love and leave the world a better place. Winning will become a byproduct of the great culture we build here at Washington Prep.

Secondly, we are selecting our team with greater concern than ever for the attitude and effort of individuals who want to be a part of the program. We are looking for loving, grateful, resilient, hardworking, and mindful individuals. While we will not look for or expect perfection, we will expect everyone to be committed to developing these virtues.

Lastly, if you were part of our summer program, you will remember that we have some non-negotiables. If you wish to have the opportunity to practice or play in games, you must:

1. *Be on time.*
2. *Listen.*
3. *Compete!*

My greatest hope for this season is that we can build a culture in which your love for the game, each other, and yourselves will grow every day. I look forward to you joining me on that journey.

Sincerely,

Daniel

At the bottom of each letter, Daniel took the time to write a personal handwritten note to each of his players, letting them know he appreciated the opportunity to coach them this upcoming season, which was a line from his favorite coach, Gregg Popovich. Then he took care to mail each letter directly to the players instead of passing them out at school, because he understood that getting mail was special and becoming rare in this day and age.

Before Daniel knew it, tryouts were upon them. As excited as he was, he knew one of the hardest steps to building a great team culture was selecting the team. But little did he know, this would be one of the greatest pre-season challenges he'd ever face.

CHAPTER 22

THE SELECTION

All coaches and prospective players reported to the school on a Friday afternoon, where they were to stay the entire weekend. Daniel had been studying the process of military selection programs, in particular the Navy SEAL BUD/S selection process. He now understood that it was not just about weeding out the "weak," but more importantly, it was about strengthening their commitment, developing mental toughness, and building relationships. Daniel needed to test the player's mindset, not just his ability. And the best way to do that was to make things really really hard! So, he designed his own hell weekend for the prospective players. The staff gave every player a practice uniform and a book called *Fearless* by Eric Blehm. Daniel then huddled the team in a very close circle in the locker room.

"Thank you all for being on time, giving us your undivided attention, and being ready to compete. Over the next few days, we are all going to try to push ourselves harder than we have ever pushed ourselves, to test our limits. You all are capable, and we believe in every one of you. But if you decide this isn't for you at any stage, you are allowed to turn in your jersey and go home. We will respect your decision."

The eyes of all twenty-four players grew wide, and he could sense some of the nervous energy permeating throughout the room. "Remember, we are looking for players who are loving, resilient, hardworking, grateful,

and mindful. None of us are perfect—especially me! You all know that."
Daniel and the other coaches chuckled, which seemed to draw a few smiles
from the players. "We need to see every second of our life, no matter how
challenging, as an opportunity to learn and grow in character."

Then Daniel had every player take a seat in the locker room and take
off their shoes. He proceeded to show them how to correctly put on their
socks without any wrinkles to prevent blisters. Then he taught them how to
tie their laces tightly and tuck their shirts in. Daniel wanted to ensure they
looked professional even at practice. Many players joked that they would
be just fine if all they had to do was tie their shoes and tuck in their shirts
this weekend!

They kicked off first practice with a series of drills, testing their various
skills of the game. The coaches recorded each player's number and success
rate in each of the drills. After the practice seemed to be coming to a close,
nearly every player was drenched in sweat. Many felt they had given it
their all. The coaches then brought in four long training sandbags meant to
be carried by four to six people. Broken into four groups, the players had
to work as a team to carry it down the court and back as fast as they could
eighty times, to represent the eighty possessions they'd likely average over
the course of a full game. If they dropped the bag, they had to start the
"possession" over. Players struggled to get in rhythm, carrying the heavy
bags awkwardly. Some groups fought, but most realized they were best
served if they all gave their best effort and worked together.

At the end of the first practice, they huddled close together, and Daniel
asked just one question: "What went well today?" He thanked each player
who shared a response. After the team spent the next fifteen minutes
going through a routine of yoga movements and deep breathing exercises,
Daniel asked everyone to pull out the book. They started by reading the
first few chapters of the story of an unlikely Navy SEAL war hero. While
many of the kids were hesitant at first, they soon became gripped by the
story, made connections to their own lives, and felt inspired for whatever
was coming tomorrow.

In the morning, when it came time for everyone to be on the court, the coaching staff only counted twenty-two players. When asked where the other two were, Eddie spoke up: "We got everyone up and out of bed, but those guys didn't want to come. They said they were too sore and needed sleep." Daniel thanked Eddie and the team for not only being on time, but for doing their best to ensure everyone else got there on time as well.

The focus of the second practice was testing their tactical play through small side-games built around executing offensive and defensive actions. Once again, the coaches kept score and recorded the results, but this time they were put in a variety of small groups of three to four players. Coaches didn't just observe the games, but also took notes on the attitude of each player, the way they treated one another, their level of effort, and how they handled mistakes or setbacks when they occurred.

At one stage, many players seemed to get so competitive they started talking trash, throwing cheap shots, and complaining about calls. So, Daniel called them together and offered a powerful principle they would be reminded of many times that season: "True competition is striving together to be your best, not to be better than somebody else. When we compete with the right spirit, we will grow closer as a team, not fall apart."

As practice came to a close, they finished with more group conditioning activities, wherein each group had a certain number of sprints, push-ups, and rebounds to grab in a certain amount of time. Aaron and Dennis tired quickly and really let up on their effort, causing the other players in their group to pick up the slack. As hard as it was, they were still able to get by after only a few attempts at the small group drill. As the morning practice ended, they stretched, did mindfulness breathing, and read a few chapters of their book as a team. They then headed to breakfast. There, they all sat along a very large table, where Daniel and the coaches strategically put the players next to one another to encourage more unlikely conversations.

As the players took naps after breakfast, the coaches gathered to plan their afternoon session. Mark, who still seemed unsure of his decision to remain on the staff, spoke first. "I get that you want to make it hard, but we had two talented underclassmen quit already. With a few more sessions left to go, we might lose some of our better players. We're selecting them for a high school basketball team, not the Navy SEALs."

Daniel nodded. "You bring up a great point, and please continue to challenge me on that. Because, to be honest, I'm unsure whether we're going too hard. Still, I know they're capable of everything we're asking of them. By raising the standards and expectations, we are letting them know we believe in them. Research shows that when cadets go through hellish training, their brains convince them that they must value what they are doing. It increases levels of commitment, connection, and loyalty to the collective team."

Fred added, "It's our job right now to continue to believe in them, encourage them, and let them know they can overcome the challenges, but only as a team! Nobody can do it on their own."

The afternoon session came quicker than any of the players would have liked. The coaches put the players into teams of five and created different game scenarios in which they were expected to compete. Often, they didn't designate a leader, but they assigned the task of coming up with an offensive and defensive strategy. After each game, they did mini after-action reviews wherein they could point out what went well but were also encouraged to speak up about what went wrong and offer solutions. Every player breathed a sigh of relief when they were told they didn't have any extra conditioning—just stretching, breathing, and reading.

Afterward, they were split into teams and tasked with preparing some part of the dinner. While they were excited not to have a conditioning session, they soon realized the difficulty of cooking for a large group of people! Still, they appreciated their meal like never before, as they had prepared it with their own hands.

After a relaxing evening as a team, the coaches told the players to put on their old shoes and sweats, because they were going outside. This would be quite a test for the team. Not as individuals or in small groups, but as a collective team. Daniel had hired a former Navy SEAL named Jocko to put them through a small simulation of BUD/S training, and the coaches were all joining in with the players.

Over the next two hours, they were given a series of team-oriented physical tasks. Without the collective effort, the tasks would be impossible. On many occasions, Daniel doubted whether they were capable of pushing through the pain and the struggle. To his surprise, every time failure seemed imminent, one young man would step up and push the team through. As the evening came to a close, Daniel dreaded making cuts the next day, because nearly every young man had not only pushed through incredibly challenging training, but had also grown closer to his fellow teammates and coaching staff.

Before going to bed, they stretched and read, but this time, each coach and many of the players shared their favorite moment from the weekend and something they learned during their training. Some players were emotional, as they had never felt so accepted or part of a family like the one they felt forming around them.

The players scrimmaged for the entirety of two hours on the last morning of tryouts. The coaches sat back and allowed the kids to organize, referee, and coach the scrimmages themselves—something Daniel believed kids had lost the skill of doing due to so many organized sports in today's society. As they watched the team, they discussed as a staff who would make the final roster of fifteen. Five players quit over the course of the weekend; some walked out, some just quietly left, and one player angrily stormed out, accusing Daniel of having lost his mind.

The coaches ranked the players. They discussed the results of the skills and competitions and were able to rank the players based on various skill and ability levels of the game. Then each coach evaluated the players on the core values.

At the end of their discussion, they agreed on the four players they'd cut. It was disappointing to cut three of the players because of their intangibles, but they made their decision based on their talent level, fitness, and skill. The final decision came down to a choice between two players: Scott or Aaron.

Fred spoke first. "Scott has a strong mindset, and we all rate him high on our core values. While he is the least talented of the last sixteen, I can bet you that will not be the case at the end of the season."

"But the disparity in the talent level between him and Aaron is miles apart," Mark scoffed. "Aaron is our best player, and even if he doesn't put in any effort, he will still be one of our best at the end of the year! It's crazy not only to think of cutting him, but to cut him to make room for Scott!"

Taylor and Chad looked at each other, unsure what to say next. Chad finally spoke up. "It's one thing to say we value something or to believe in mindset, but sitting here and facing this decision and then having to live according to that truth is a whole other thing. I would rather spend the next year coaching Scott, if this is based solely on the experience."

Taylor hesitated. "I agree, but Aaron didn't quit this weekend. His attitude was by far the worst, but he didn't quit. Don't we have a duty to serve and love these kids despite their imperfections?"

Fred chimed back in. "Nobody is more important than the team, no matter how good they are. Talented individuals do not automatically guarantee great results. A selfish mindset will infect this culture, and Aaron has one."

Daniel nodded as every coach spoke. "You all have made great points, and I don't disagree with any of them. Our choice will create our challenge. And I can't help but think this decision will send a really big message to the players about what we value the most. We reinforce what we value. And some values are worth dying for, so they are definitely worth breaking up over. Aaron has been in the program for three years, and we have done our best to love and serve him. But it's time for me to start valuing my values."

"What the hell? You can't seriously be about to cut one of the best players in the city who just stuck out two grueling days of tryouts for you and this team!" Mark shouted. "I'm not going to stand by and let this happen. If he's gone, I'm gone." And with that, stormed out of the coaches' office.

As the players finished up, showered, and got ready for the team lunch, the coaches called each and every player into their office to let them know if they made the team. They also took that time to select those they believed should be part of a leadership group they were forming.

When it came time to let Aaron know he didn't make the team, Daniel got straight to it. "Aaron, you have played for me for the last three years, but I have decided it is in the best interest of the program if you move on and start getting ready for your college football career. As far as you have come and as talented as you are, your personal goals and level of commitment are not in alignment with the expectations and vision for our team."

Tears welled up in Aaron's eyes. "I've never been cut before in my life ... I can't believe you would do this to me. You really are as stupid as they say you are." And with that, he walked right out of the office.

To cap off their weekend, the players all worked together to cook an amazing lunch for the team and their parents. The whole team and all their parents sat in tables positioned in one large circle across the cafeteria. Having their kids cook for them blew the parents away! As the meal came to a close, Daniel went to the front of the table, called up each player to receive his jersey, and said a few encouraging words about each one.

Finally, Daniel called up Kevin, Eddie, and Archie, the captains selected by the team. While he would intentionally work to develop leaders in every player, he decided to follow the legendary All Blacks rugby team in creating a leadership group, not only to lean on, but also to pass on responsibility throughout the season.

> **Reflect and write: How can you implement a "selection process" to test your team's mindset while bringing them together and strengthening commitment to the team?**

Daniel lost one of his most talented players and a great coach over hell weekend. But he had no regrets. He finally was practicing what he preached. Only time would tell if this experiment would actually work, but

Daniel felt confident that he had assembled a team of young men willing to buy into the process and fight like hell for their teammates. That alone was enough to put a smile on Daniel's face.

CHAPTER 23

CREATE A SHARED VISION AND PURPOSE

After the long hard weekend of training and the jersey ceremony, every member of the team—coaches included—felt confident this was a special group of people. As they walked the halls the following Monday at school, they started talking about their goals for the upcoming season. Many players bragged about how good they were going to be. A few players even sent out some tweets about a state championship in their sights! Daniel knew trouble was brewing the second he got wind of this. It reminded him of when he climbed Clearview Mountain, and the resulting danger of setting his eyes on the peak and not what was in front of him.

Regardless, exhausted and sore from the long weekend, Daniel knew his players could use a day of physical rest. So, he booked a hotel conference room, ordered some food, and gathered the team there that evening to focus on their mindset.

As the team sat in groups of three to four players, each around their own small table, the coaches passed out notebooks and pens to each of them. They all felt like they were attending some high-powered business meeting, and some of the kids even made lighthearted jokes about it.

Daniel addressed the team. "Who here wants to win a state title?"

The energy in the room surged, players smiled, and every last hand flew up. Daniel smiled in response. "What if the State Athletic Association came in here today, right this very minute, and presented you with the trophy? Would you be happy?" Puzzled looks covered the room.

"How about you, Eddie?"

Eddie shrugged and said, "Well, I guess it wouldn't mean anything; the trophy would just be a piece of wood and metal."

Daniel's eyes lit up. "Exactly, Eddie! A trophy in and of itself means nothing. You all want to *earn* a championship, not be given one. See, it's not about the destination, but about the journey—the experience. Isn't it?" Every player in the room nodded his head.

Daniel continued, "I have given you each a notebook. This is your notebook for the entire season, so take good care of them. While you eat dinner today in your groups, I want you to discuss the answers to some very important questions: Why have we succeeded in the past? Why have we failed? You all have been a part of this program or other programs before, so your ideas are just as good as our ideas."

As the coaches ate their dinner, Daniel let them know what he was thinking. "They may throw out some off-the-wall ideas today, but we should not only listen, but be willing to concede and negotiate on certain things. We need them to know that this is not my team or your team at the end of the day. Rather, it's *our* team. We all have a say. Jim McGuinness, a legendary Irish football coach, did something like this with his team. It was one of the most influential team meetings I have ever read about, and I instantly knew we could do the same thing to empower our players."

As the players ate, they talked about the problems they had faced in the past and tried to find solutions to each of them. After everyone finished dinner, they took the time to write everything down. Daniel and the coaches remained seated but asked every group to come up, write down their solutions on the whiteboard, and then share them with the team. Players pointed out everything from off-the-court activities and warm-up drills before games to offensive strategies and some good and bad practice habits.

After each group presented, Daniel came to the front of the room and said, "I know you all have big dreams. Dreams that have been in your hearts for a long time. Some of you have set big goals. Those goals and dreams can be the fuel to drive your efforts and help you move forward, but our focus needs to be on our purpose. Our mission. Why do we play basketball? What can we do to live our journey?"

Daniel went on to share the mission of several famous people and his own mission for coaching. Each group came up with a mission of their own, and the team voted to select the mission they would adopt.

Then Daniel asked them to think of their greatest teammate ever. "What qualities did you admire most about the person? What made them an exceptional teammate?" They wrote these qualities down and shared with the team. Then they selected the top four qualities as the values—or pillars—on which to build the program.

Next, Daniel asked what principles or mantras they had learned that could help them make sure they were on track with each of the values they chose. They needed a blueprint to build a "house" that lined up with their values—their pillars. The small groups came up with a variety of principles while the coaches mingled and helped. Afterward, they discussed each value and shared a principle they thought would be necessary.

When it came to commitments, they looked at the long list they had written on the whiteboard. It included a variety of reasons why they had or hadn't been successful in the past. Daniel then posed three questions to the team.

1. What do we need to start doing?
2. What do we need to stop doing?
3. What do we need to keep doing?

"Let's come up with various commitments that are controllable and measurable in every aspect of our program," he said. "How will you know when you have been successful?" Together, they discussed, shared, and finalized a definition of a successful team. Daniel gave them a few minutes and asked one of the players to write all of this on the whiteboard. After a few minutes, the whiteboard was covered with the following:

....

The Washington Prep Warriors Team Manifesto

<u>Success</u>: Giving our best in everything we do.
<u>Mission</u>: Love work, love play, love each other.
<u>Values</u>: A caring attitude, hard work, competi-
tiveness, and grit.

<u>Principles</u>:

1. Treat others the way you want to be treated.
2. Hard work beats talent when talent fails to work hard.
3. It's not about the size of the dog in the fight, but the size of the fight in the dog.
4. It's not about how hard you can hit; it's about how hard you can get hit and keep moving forward.

<u>Commitments</u>:

1. Before practice, we will acknowledge and greet every teammate.
2. During practice, we will high-five every teammate and make at least one "hustle" play each.
3. After practice, we will make four free throws in a row before leaving the gym, and we will thank a teammate and a coach for their effort.
4. Before games, we will put our phones on airplane mode or turn them off one hour before tip-off.

5. During games, we will always stand for subs, and when we are subbed off, we will high-five everyone on the bench.
6. After games, we will not leave until we have pointed out one thing that went well in the game.
7. When we have an injury, we will get to the training room with plenty of time to make it to practice.
8. As a team, we will clean the locker room after every practice and game.
9. In school, we will all request to sit in the front of the classroom, and we will keep a notebook of our homework and upcoming tests.
10. We will communicate all practice and game times to our parents at home.
11. We will post only things that represent the mission and core values of the team on social media.
12. We will not drink any soda in season.
13. We will plan and schedule to get a minimum of seven hours of sleep every night, and we will not have our phones in bed.
14. Everyone must do at least one thirty-minute individual or partner workout a week outside of practice.
15. At team functions, we will dress appropriately and speak appropriately.
16. At team meals, we will all be thankful and display great manners.

17. We will lift weights twice a week in season for thirty minutes.
18. We will serve the community in a team service project once a month.

Daniel asked all the players to take out their cellphones after they completed the exercise. "You should each take a picture of this and post it on your favorite social media site. Take selfies with it, group photos, whatever. Make it the background for our home-screen or computer. I don't care. What's important to me is you keep this close to you at all times and check it as a reminder of your vision and commitments for this season."

It only took a few seconds for every player to pull out a cell phone and crowd around the whiteboard. Daniel and his coaches looked on as the team buzzed with excitement, totally oblivious to the challenges about to present themselves.

Reflect and write: Before you create a manifesto, consider whose team it is. Whose experience is more important—you as a leader or the members of your team?

CHAPTER 24

BUILD AN INTRINSICALLY MOTIVATED CULTURE

Daniel arrived early to observe the players enter the gym to begin their warm-ups before the first official practice of the season started. Many of the players seemed to ignore each other, especially Archie. Only a few said hello to all the coaches and players. On top of that, Archie was the last to stroll in and headed straight for the basket where Eddie and Kevin, his best friends, were standing. Daniel shrugged it off.

Things seemed to be going well as practice got going, but Archie once again let up on effort as soon as the drills or small games seemed uninteresting to him. This proved to be contagious throughout the team. Daniel was furious! It was as if they had completely forgotten the commitments they'd made the day before.

Daniel, growing more and more irritated, called the team together to chew them out. "What level is our effort at as a team?" he barked. "Who has made a hustle play? How many people have high-fived a teammate?" They were less questions for his team to ponder and more judgments about what had just occurred. And while practice effort seemed to pick up ever so slightly, it quickly fizzled out yet again.

Daniel sat in his office after everyone had left. In the post-practice meeting, he had asked the players and coaches to point out things that went wrong and then offer up some solutions. Everyone identified a lack of effort and focus, but many of the suggestions seemed to fall flat, except for two comments.

First, in the after-action review, a player named Matthew said, "Today felt a lot different than yesterday. We were so close last night, but then today, I felt distant from some of my teammates. It didn't feel as special." Daniel reflected on this comment only to realize he had let their commitment slide.

Secondly, in the coaches meeting, the young assistant coach Taylor said, "When you called everyone together and asked those questions, it didn't seem like they were questions. I really saw a big drop in the team's energy after that." Daniel embraced the painful feedback and thought about how the two issues might be related to his problem. As he looked through his notes, he realized: *enforce healthy boundaries and consequences with love.* The boys had made a commitment; he needed to remind them of that commitment and do it from a place of love.

It seemed like even fewer people made the effort to greet each other before practice the next day. But Daniel would have none of it. He called the team together at the start of the practice and said, "We all committed to starting practice on a great note by acknowledging each other and saying hello. I could have done a better job of this as well. We do not start practice until everyone has done this, because we want this to be a great practice. Let's try this again. Everyone, leave the gym and practice reentering the *right* way." Everyone awkwardly walked out of the gym. Daniel put up three minutes on the clock, and the players walked back in as if the last ten minutes had never happened. He wanted them to feel like they were starting over.

This instantly sparked a positive practice—different from how it had been the day before. The team showed a higher level of energy from the start and things moved along well until the midway point, when Archie seemed content to find a reason to "stretch out" during almost every defensive drill. Instead of ignoring it, Daniel employed some transformational discipline. When he failed to pick it up, Daniel quickly and calmly reprimanded him, reminding him of the consequences for not competing. Still, his words seemed to fall on deaf ears. So this time Daniel did not hesitate to let him know he had lost the privilege to practice.

While Archie stormed out of the practice, the rest of the team seemed to instantly elevate their level of effort. Daniel didn't know it then, but it would be the last time in a long time he would have to enforce that consequence with a player!

As hard and as focused as the team was, Daniel and his coaches still knew the players were holding back. Practices were still too comfortable, and their play was too clean-looking. He knew they needed to train ugly, not pretty.

Over the years, Daniel had worked hard to extrinsically motivate his teams. At first, it was the old-school approach: "If you all don't work hard, then we will run until you pass out!" But Daniel was smarter now and understood that was leading with fear. One time, Fred, his old-school assistant, had encouraged him to just run them into the ground the day after a bad game, but Daniel stood strong and said, "I would rather inspire them to work harder than control them with fear."

As the years moved on, he tried to be more "positive" and even created a rewards system. Players could score points that they could use later to get protein bars and Gatorades when they won games or did little intangibles. While this was effective in the short term, it was not effective in the long term, because he now understood they only performed for a reward. Just as the science showed, those rewards lost their effect as players started to cheat in games, take shortcuts, want greater rewards, and lost sight of the big picture.

Luckily, he had studied the science behind extrinsic and intrinsic motivation in the off-season. Before the first practice, Daniel had worked to create that intrinsically motivated environment, which comes from autonomy, mastery, and purpose.

Reflect and write: What steps can you take to offer autonomy to your team? Do you feel as if your team members can see and feel their growth? Are your

team members connected to a purpose greater than themselves?

....

While he had his own non-negotiables, he gave the team the *autonomy* to define their core values and make the commitments necessary to be successful. He enforced consequences and reminded them that it was their choice not to meet the standards.

The team started to build meaningful relationships and actually identified a purpose of serving something greater than themselves. Still, after the second day, he realized he had ignored the element of *mastery*. The team was training with a fixed mindset, afraid of failure. How could he help them overcome the fear of mistakes? As he watched the practice video, he noticed that the coaching staff was not working together. Not only did they point out every mistake, but sometimes, two or three coaches would get on a player. No wonder these kids were afraid of making mistakes!

The next practice, Daniel apologized for being overly critical and then explained why and how he was going to change his approach to coaching during practices. "I want you to be competitive, but I want you to compete to get better, not so you feel better than somebody else." Daniel then showed them a brief video about "deliberate practice," explaining that it was necessary to be outside your comfort zone and work on the edge of your abilities, and that it would require them to make lots of mistakes!

After that, he started by showing a few videos of how a talented college team executed an offensive set. Instead of sharing the teaching points with them, he asked, "Why is this important?" After they shared good reasons, he asked, "What three things do we need to do well to execute that fundamental or play?"

They then ran through the play without any opposition, and eventually added some other players into the mix. The coaches didn't criticize them for their mistakes, but instead asked the players to coach themselves and watch the offensive set again and again on an iPad. The environment shifted to one where the coaches weren't just the teachers, but the players themselves also became teachers.

The players improved their intensity levels in practice, but the coaches and players still knew they could give more. Daniel had always believed in the power of competition, but in the past years he saw competition take away from the joy of play. While they kept score in nearly every small-sided game or scrimmage in the practice, there was no system of rewards and punishments. Players were *playing* hard, but it was clear they weren't *competing* hard. Daniel knew he needed to add another wrinkle.

He gathered the team close in a huddle at the start of the next practice. "Competing . . . it's not about beating someone or being better than someone else. The word actually comes from the Latin word *competo*, which means *to strive toward excellence*. Competing is about being your best and striving for excellence. Starting today, we're going to have the 'Competitors Wall,' where players will be ranked by their wins in a variety of areas in practice. Building our team is much like building a house, and we must understand that competition can either be a wedge that drives us apart, or it can be a vice clamp that brings us together! It's not about anybody losing, it's about us all striving to be our best, and getting better every practice and game. Use competition not to triumph over others, but to make us all better."

And with that, they began practice. They would chart wins in one-to-one games, three-to-three games, and five-to-five games in each practice. They charted winners in the sprint competitions, shooting competitions, and free throw competitions.

Then the coaching staff accumulated the data and updated the rankings on the board in the locker room. Daniel never spoke about the rankings again, just about the principle of competing to be at their best. The rankings were a subtle reminder and motivator, as nobody wanted to be near the bottom.

CHAPTER 25

A NEW WAY OF COMMUNICATING

O n the Saturday after the first week of practice, Daniel headed over for a long afternoon with John. As Daniel arrived, he saw that John had invited another friend. His name was Andy. After eating a fantastic lunch and spending some time getting to know each other, John said, "Well, did you bring all the practice recordings from the week?"

Daniel nodded.

"All right then; phones off, notebook out, let's get to work. I've invited Andy, a communications specialist, to help us today. We're going to get into the nitty-gritty here."

"If there's something I can do to help myself become a better coach and improve the team's chances of success, then I'm all for it."

Andy smiled. "Great to hear that, Daniel. Before we start going through the video, there are just a few things. I'm going to give you some hard feedback, but I'm giving you this feedback because I want you to succeed. I know your growth is critical to the success of the team, and a bunch of young people are counting on you. I have really high expectations when it comes to communication, but I know you can meet them."

Daniel listened as Andy continued, "I don't use sandwich feedback. You know the positive-negative-positive sandwich?" Daniel nodded. "Good. I don't use it because people either ignore all the positives or they ignore all the negatives. What I *do* use is what I call 'notifications.' Notifications are

159

not judgmental, but a simple communication of things that I observe. The other thing I do is ask a lot of questions, so be ready for those since they'll be coming at ya."

Daniel was incredibly grateful for the opportunity to have someone give him high-level feedback in a video session. Time seemed to fade away as they became completely locked into watching replays of the practices.

Andy made several observations about Daniel's body language and communication before the practice even started. "You do a great job welcoming every player by making some physical contact—by high-fiving, patting on the back, or putting your arm around them. I can tell you have worked on this and you are intentional, but still authentically engaged." Daniel smiled, feeling good. "I really like your moment of vulnerability by taking ownership for the poor practice from the day before. That's great because it's going to encourage them to take ownership of themselves and be more vulnerable."

"One thing I have learned," John chimed in, "is that ninety percent of our communication is nonverbal. Our body language—the heart posture toward your players that you have been training—is communicated far before we start talking. Andy is here to help you become more intentional in the way you communicate."

"Absolutely. I worked for years with one of the best NBA coaches of all time to help him develop this, because some of it is not natural."

Daniel interrupted, "I remember hearing Brad Stevens say his number-one piece of advice for coaches was to be yourself. If it isn't natural, then aren't we being fake?"

Andy chuckled. "Was shooting a left-handed lay-up natural to you at the start?"

"No, not at all."

"But if you wanted to be the best player you could be, you knew you needed to get better at it, right? You want to be yourself but the best version of yourself, which is who your players need. Great coaches are what their players need them to be: cheerleader or drill sergeant. Differs for many players and differs for many days of the season. Now, what else do you know about how the best leaders communicate?"

Daniel was excited to share. "Well, in Daniel Coyle's book *The Talent Code,* he discusses how nearly ever master coach he observed was quiet, reserved, and watching intently. They listened more than they talked. Carol Dweck's book, *Mindset,* discusses how we need to praise effort, not achievement, if we want them to have a growth mindset and be focused on the process."

"Well, you're quite the encyclopedia, Daniel. These are all very good principles; let's see how well you apply them." Andy played the video again. After a few minutes, he paused the video as it caught a conversation between Daniel and Archie in which Daniel said, "Archie, you are such a talented and natural defender out there; if you can be more willing to sacrifice your body for the rebound and loose balls, you will be unstoppable."

Andy looked to Daniel. "Is that the most beneficial wording you can use?"

Daniel chuckled. "No, not at all. I even remember a similar conversation my sixth grade basketball coach had with me. He told me I was a natural. My belief that I was a natural led me to believe that it would always come naturally. But it didn't. In fact, I spent thousands of hours in my backyard shooting hoops as a child, and I stopped that when people started to tell me I was 'gifted.' When I was talking to Archie, what I really meant was that he was skilled. Skilled is a much better word than talented."

"When you say something to a player," John began, "it doesn't matter what it means to you. It matters what it means to that player. That's another reason why it's important to be intentional about our language."

Andy continued playing the video, and as the players were doing a shooting drill, they listened to the coaching staff giving feedback to the players. "What are you hearing? Write it down."

So Daniel wrote down the following:
"Good shot."
"Come on and focus."
"Stop thinking so much."
"That's a lazy shot."
"Shoot it better."
"You need to get it together."
"Come on, you can do better."
"We can't miss this many free-throws and win any games!"

....

Reflect and write: Write out your favorite maxims or mantras. Which of them best represents the culture you are trying to build?

....

Andy spoke directly. "You and your coaches are not specific in your feedback. Work to avoid saying 'good job'; instead, try saying 'good follow through' or 'great balance.' Players do better when there's clarity in your notifications and commands."

Daniel jotted down notes as Andy continued, "One of the hard things is not to use controlling language. Instead of saying you 'must' or 'need to,' try saying 'consider' or 'try to' more often. I still struggle with this as well, but it's a small change that can help empower rather than control. Also, one coach said, 'stop thinking so much,' but when we tell people not to think of something, what do they do? They think of it! Instead, try telling or asking them what they should focus on."

Daniel said, "Another area I need—I mean, I *should* work on is with feedback. I'm so worried about being too critical."

John jumped into the conversation. "A great trap that many coaches and parents fall into today: false positivity. Young people see right through it, but still, there are only so many corrective comments you can make before you damage the relationship. Try to use language and build a relationship in which the player knows you are criticizing the performance, not the person. Michael Jordan's NBA coach Phil Jackson never tried to call a player selfish when they took some bad shots; instead, he would say things like, 'You were a little thirsty out there, weren't you?'"

Andy, John, and Daniel lost track of time as they went through hours of video. Mostly, Andy just asked questions, like, "What could you have done differently? What would have been a more beneficial word? What was a great moment?"

After they had gone through all the practices, Andy said to Daniel, "Remember, *what* is greater than *why*. If you notice, I didn't ask you why you did things today, I just focused on solutions and asked what you should have done. You do a good job by asking players to self-evaluate but continue to develop some power questions you can ask! The great Dick DeVenzio would ask players, 'Is the level you are practicing at right now in direct proportion to your aspirations?' Continue to develop your questions so that you're calling your players up, not out."

Daniel thanked Andy for all the time he'd spent working with him so he could be a better coach. As they got up to leave, John said, "Hold on, one more thing before we go. Don't just develop your questions and train your feedback, but create your own language. I had my list of maxims that I would use time and time again. Short phrases that sent a strong message without having to talk a lot. 'Be quick; don't hurry.' 'Happiness begins where selfishness ends.' 'Earn the right to be proud.' These are some just to name a few."

Daniel nodded and said, "Just like the All Blacks rugby team: 'Sweep the sheds.' 'Go for the gap.' And the Marines: 'Once a Marine, always a Marine.' And the San Antonio Spurs: 'Pound the rock.'"

Andy chuckled. "Boy, you know your stuff. Keep learning, keep training, and keep taking small steps forward. You might even think about putting up those mantras and maxims on the walls of your locker room.

CHAPTER 26
WORK WITH PARENTS

It didn't take long for Daniel to feel pressure from the players' parents. Aaron's father and grandparents had contacted the athletic director and school principal to discuss exactly why he did not make the team. They even garnered some support from a few other parents, who complained and immediately requested a coaching change "before the season got out of hand." However, to the surprise of Daniel and the other coaches, his fellow teammates didn't miss Aaron, or at least, if they did, they didn't speak up about it.

Daniel enforced boundaries in the first week, preventing Dennis from practicing and even asking Archie to leave at one point. Both boys didn't fight it or put up much resistance, and instead apologized the next day to the whole team. But their parents didn't share these same sentiments.

Dennis's father drove to the school before Daniel could leave after practice and proceeded to yell at him for over fifteen minutes. "How dare you sit my son out of practice after all he has done for you and this program? He's only a fifteen-year-old boy; you can't expect him to be 'perfect' and communicate. He barely even speaks to *me*. The parents and I are tired of you and your crazy philosophies; just go ahead and leave because you're going to be fired anyway!"

Archie's mother sent a vicious email to Daniel that very night, accusing him of always picking on her son and threatening to pull him from the team if he was "kicked" out of practice once again.

Could this get any worse? Daniel thought as he got into bed, only to receive a text from Scott's dad, who had been one of his few constant supporters during his time at the school. The text read: *Coach, I'm never one to send this type of message; I don't like to be that type of parent, so please don't mention this to Scott, but I think he's really struggling lately, and I'm worried. He just doesn't talk to us much anymore. I think he's worried this will be another year that he doesn't get to play much. I hope you will appreciate his commitment to the program all this time, and hopefully you will realize he has earned that starting spot.*

Daniel's heart sunk, because Scott—as good of a kid as he was—had not worked hard this off-season and was not going to be good enough to even come off the bench for meaningful minutes in all likelihood.

Daniel didn't sleep a wink that night, tossing and turning with great worry. Had he totally screwed this up? Why did he even bother coming back? Were the parents right? Should he just quit?

Things only seemed to get worse the next day, as he had yet another meeting with the administration to reassure them he wasn't crossing any lines with how hard he was working the boys. After a good practice that night, Daniel was getting into his car when he saw Dennis sitting on a bench. "Hey, Dennis, you need a ride?"

"No, I'm good," he replied.

"When are your parents going to get here?"

"I'm not sure; my dad had a job interview this evening."

Daniel put the car into park and said, "Get in; I'll take you home." Dennis got into the car, and they made the twenty-minute trek to a rough part of the city. Two things quickly became apparent to Daniel as they were driving along. First, Dennis didn't share his dad's anger or frustration from the previous day but was almost appreciative of Daniel for enforcing the boundaries. Secondly, Dennis's home life was a mess.

Dennis started to cry as they pulled up to the apartments. "I don't want to go in there. I'm tired of their fighting. My mom blames my dad for losing his job, and she's threatening to leave him—to leave *us*. It's not my dad's fault he lost his job, and my mom has been so horrible to him for so long. I know she has someone else on the side as well. Coach, I hate this place and I cannot wait to leave."

Daniel was stunned. He didn't know what to say, and the only thing that seemed to come out was, "I'm so sorry you have to go through that. I'm here for you if you ever need to talk some more." And with that, Dennis dried his eyes and hopped out of the car.

As Daniel drove home, it hit him: the parents were not disrespectful, unappreciative, and rude to him because of *him*, they were doing those things because of who *they* were and what they were going through. As hard as it was, he couldn't keep taking those attacks personally, and he had to stop seeing parents as obstacles, but instead as people who needed love as well.

Daniel arrived home and shared with his wife, Brownie, what seemed like an "impossible battle" with the parents. Brownie said, "Who has been the greatest influence on you and your character?"

"My parents, without a doubt."

Brownie smiled. "Exactly! And that's what the majority of people say when you ask them the same question. Family is the first school of character; it's where we learn about love. It's where we develop a work ethic, resilience, and gratitude. As big of an impact as you can have on a child's life, the most effective people for doing that is their family; don't forget that. And it's not just your kids from tougher socio-economic backgrounds. Wealthy parents can be so highly demanding but emotionally distant at the same time, creating a sense of hopelessness and shame."

"If I'm going to build a transformational culture, I'll need to figure out a way to work with the parents to help build it. Things will work way better if we support each other."

Brownie smiled. "You're starting to get it. I hear coaches and teachers complain about the newest generation of kids and parents, but they continue with the same approach. Always expecting the parents to change. We need to change our approach to see these 'overly involved' parents as an opportunity. What if you got the parents to buy into the team mission as well? What if you used your platform as the coach to help educate and empower the parents to be better?" After their talk, Daniel made his way upstairs and opened his laptop.

———

Everyone thought Daniel had lost his mind when they saw his email. The coaches, the players, and even the parents thought he was crazy.

To All Parents,

I think we can all agree that nobody on either side enjoys the parent-coach meeting at the start of the season. Well, let's change that. This Sunday, I'd like to invite you to join us for practice. We encourage you to wear your athletic shoes and clothes and participate as much as possible. Afterward, my wife and the other coaches' wives will be cooking a great meal for coaches, players, and parents to share together. Finally, we will meet to discuss the upcoming season and how we can create a great experience for everyone: players, coaches, and parents alike.

Sincerely,

Daniel

Nearly every parent attended the practice and nearly every family had at least one parent participate in the practice. Everything about it felt uncomfortable and awkward at first, but it was only a matter of minutes before the parents started smiling and laughing as they rekindled their love for basketball. Their children were encouraged to step up and coach them during some of the drills and games. Sometimes, the parents just sat back and watched the players go through some of the tougher drills. It proved to be a blast, as they finished with some exciting scrimmages that included the parents and a few game-winning shots.

Next, the families gathered for an amazing dinner prepared by the coaches' wives. All of the coaches' children attended as well, and it was special to have everyone together. It helped them see each other in a different light. Daniel was very intentional about the seating and made sure to place people where they had the opportunity to mix and talk with each other.

The most challenging thing about the experience was that Daniel had to readjust his heart posture toward the parents who had "wronged" him in the past. He smiled, welcomed them, and even said quietly to a few, "I hope you can give me the opportunity to put things on a better footing."

> **Reflect and write: How can you help create a transformational experience for the parents?**

Daniel started the actual meeting the same way he tried to start every important meeting—with a little bit of vulnerability. "I know that I've been an imperfect coach in the past, and I will continue to make mistakes, but I want you to know that I'm not only trying to serve these young men by becoming a better leader, but I want to find ways to support all of you in your most challenging life task—that of parenting."

After admitting some of his imperfections, he went on to share his coaching manifesto with the parents, along with his mission, core values, and guiding principles. He stressed the importance of modeling this and not just being all talk. He shared some areas where he struggled to do that. Then he gave every parent three notecards and asked them some very important questions that not only gave the parents a voice but encouraged them to think about how they could help create a transformational experience for the team.

Next, he said that he had made some changes to his former "policies." He recommended that a parent should not be too quick to contact him about playing time, roles, strategy, or the other kids, but that if they were really bothered by something—even those topics—he would rather they talk to him about it instead of with the other parents or their sons. He told them to email him their concerns and he would appropriately respond either by email, a phone call, or a meeting.

Finally, Daniel asked the parents for their help and offered his support in three areas. "First, enforce boundaries and consequences for your child. If you believe they have not lived up to your standards academically or behaviorally, or even that they have not done their chores around the house, I support you a hundred percent in making them sit out a practice or a game. We need to work together to make them see basketball as a privilege, not an entitlement. Secondly, please work with me to help model the character and sportsmanship we want them to display. We must be the people we want them to become. Thirdly, support them in their struggle, but let them struggle. It's the hardest thing we must do as parents—letting them struggle and experience adversity. But it helps them learn to deal with conflict, assert themselves, and develop resilience."

As Daniel scanned the room, he felt a sense of relief and satisfaction. If only for one night, it appeared that everyone was on the same page, and he could feel a tremendous sense of togetherness. While Daniel still had a lot of work to do to unite the parents and their children with his goals and change in approach, he was satisfied that this evening was a good start.

For more ideas on building a unique parent meeting be sure to get the Calling Up Coach's Guide at **thriveonchallenge.com.**

CHAPTER 27

BUILD A CULTURE MANUAL

Daniel sat in his office, feeling completely overwhelmed. His desk was covered with books, notebooks, and Post-it notes with little reminders on them. Over the last six months he had compiled an incredible wealth of resources and learned so much. But even then, applying it all was way harder than knowing it all. After his video session with John and Andy, he was worried about whether he would ever become a master coach. He knew he had to be intentional about building the culture of the team—a selfless culture in which everyone was ready to sacrifice for the greater good. Everything looked great on paper, but could they turn that into action, create habits, and build virtue? He didn't feel like he had enough time to do even half of what he wanted to do.

As he leaned back in his chair, he noticed an email come in from a guy named Dustin. The subject was "Time Management 101." It was clearly one of those mass emails sent to millions of people and then forwarded on and on. *Still, this might be worth a look*, Daniel thought as he opened the email to see a story written within.

A college professor was standing in front of his class. As class began, he held up a large jar full of rocks. He then asked the class if it was full. All the students agreed that it was.

Next, he took a box of pebbles and poured them into the jar and shook the jar around, so the pebbles fell into the open areas. All the students smiled. *"Now is it full?" he asked. The students hesitated and, without as much conviction as before, said, "Yes."*

Then the professor picked up a bag of sand and poured it into the jar, and the jar filled up with sand. "Now is it full?" The jar looked packed tight, and all the students said, "Yes, it has to be full now!"

But then the professor took the glass of water he had been drinking and poured the water into the jar. The students laughed.

The professor smiled and said, "The jar is representative of the time in your life. Eighty-six thousand, four hundred seconds in your day. Your week. Your months. Your years. What are you going to fill it with? First, start with your priorities—your rocks—then add your pebbles—smaller, but still important things. Then add the sand—the things that are good to do, but not essential. Lastly, add the water—the fun and easy things to do. Manage your time in this way, take care of your priorities first, and you will be amazed at how much fuller of a life you can live.

Daniel started to think. *What are the rocks in our program? Culture.* He decided to lay out an intentional season plan that would maintain their priorities. *The way we spend our time will say what we value. We need to prioritize our time and build daily disciplines and weekly traditions to live this out.*

He shared this idea with his assistants as they gathered for their weekly coaches meeting. Together, they brainstormed a way to organize their days and weeks so everyone—coaches included—would be held accountable. They would start small but revisit the plan every week by dedicating time to each coaches' weekly review and progress session, making any necessary tweaks, as well as adding a few more disciplines.

Fred, who was the manager of a hospital, enthusiastically spoke up. "Did you know that a group of researchers found a procedure recently that saved over fifteen hundred lives, saved them nearly a hundred million dollars, and reduced infection by over sixty percent? Guess what it was?" Everyone paused, expecting some big reveal. "A checklist. One thing I wanted to bring up was how messy we leave our locker room and the gym after practices. I would like to create a checklist for all members on the team to help them build the habit of cleaning up after themselves."

"I love it! Let's make sure they are cleaning water bottles, the gym, the locker room, and doing the laundry," Daniel said. "We need to clean up more than the trash in our locker room, though." For years, Daniel had let the "locker room" talk slide, because he felt it was important to let boys be boys. Sure, he knew he had been just as bad—if not worse—when it came to cursing, making cutting remarks to his teammates, and making degrading comments about women. Daniel and the staff believed it was time to reshape the locker room to make it a place where character and virtue were built through the behaviors they modeled and their language, but also through what they read, wrote about, the stories they told, and the discussions they had.

Daniel finished off the meeting with a new challenge to his staff. "Now, we need to build our culture manual. So we can intentionally build a culture of character, selflessness, and great leaders. Our culture manual will be the plan to do that!"

The team started working on a success log after practice together. The team leaders would go to the dry-erase board and write down the things people felt they did well in practice. The coaches knew that the stories we tell ourselves become our beliefs, and they wanted to instill this into the root of their team. What we believe determines our perception of the world. People need to be trained to see the good, because life has conditioned them to see the bad. Only after they wrote down five things they did well could they write down one area for growth and one action they could take to improve in that area.

During the selection process, Daniel had seen the power of reading as a team. All great teams have their own compelling story, and he knew that listening to the stories of people who had persevered was a powerful message to impart to the team. Every day after practice, the team would read a short chapter or section from a book that would take under five minutes.

Stories went beyond what they read, as guest speakers came in on a weekly basis. Role models from the community and alumni shared how their stories connected to the core values of the team. Not only was it great for the kids, but the speakers appreciated the opportunity, and it strengthened the program's relationships with alumni and the community.

> **Reflect and write: Think of one small intentional step you can take to start training the following: character, mental toughness, and leadership.**

Daniel coined Wednesdays as "Wisdom Wednesdays," and the team finished practice fifteen minutes early so they could listen to a presentation from a member of the coaching staff on an important topic each week. Topics varied from controversial news issues and social issues to guidelines for dating, eating manners, and even personal hygiene tips like shaving and clipping their nails.

As competitive as their practices grew, Daniel knew that sometimes the competitive cauldron would not be enough to mimic the high levels of stress that came within a game. Research has shown that practicing under stress is necessary to prepare people to perform in the big moments and keep them from choking. Nearly every practice, Daniel used the Navy SEALs "Pays to Be a Winner" method, in which the winning team in a competition didn't have to do any extra conditioning. Just like the competitive cauldron, he took the time to explain the purpose behind this.

"The winning team will be exempt from the conditioner, but the conditioning for the teams that don't finish first is not a 'punishment,' it's just a tool to help us sharpen our skills by creating more pressure. It's important that we all understand why we are doing this. In the end, everyone is a winner because the conditioning will be good for the weaker teams."

Daniel copied the All Blacks rugby team's training system, in which the games would often require the teams to perform after already reaching the point of exhaustion in a practice, and would require them to step up, lead, and problem solve as a team to call the right play and execute it. Daniel worked to train a team that could think under pressure, especially when they were tired.

Daniel hoped that in future seasons he could build a culture that would employ football coach Jim Harbaugh's rule of winner's run, which reinforces that athletes should want to do extra conditioning because it's good for them. But for now, he just followed up and finished the practice with a toughness sprint conditioner. Every player would finish a sprint, but instead of the traditional "first is out," he modified it to "last is out first." Suddenly, it turned into a competition to see who would be the last man standing. As players got "out," they stood on the sidelines and cheered on the remaining players. The more the team ran, the more they believed in the benefits of conditioning.

As helpful as these mental training activities were, players still got upset, fell into ruts, and could get an attitude at times. After a while, Daniel knew he needed to devise a trigger to help players move from the uncontrollables to the controllables. When a player's focus shifted in practice, or a player fell into a rut, cocked an attitude, or got upset, one of the coaches would just say, "ACT, don't react."

Daniel called his team together before one practice and said, "Fellas, mental toughness is the ability to move your focus from the uncontrollables to the controllables. It's not easy to do this when things don't go the way we hoped, and it's natural to focus on things outside of our control, which is why we need to train our mental toughness. When I say to you, 'ACT, don't react,' what I'm saying is that you need to: A—be aware of your feelings and focus, C—compose yourself by focusing on the controllables, and T—take action on the controllables."

That very practice, Archie lost his cool after he felt he was fouled on a drive to the basket. He walked back on defense, gave up a rebound, then turned the ball over on the next play. Daniel called a time-out.

"Archie, come over here." Daniel put his arm around him as he said, "ACT, don't react. What are you focused on?"

Archie's shoulders slumped. "The fact that I didn't get a foul call."

"Now, what can you control?"

"Getting back and playing hard defense."

Daniel smiled. "So take action!"

Archie picked up his head and sprinted back onto the court.

Daniel and the coaching staff used this method of correction with great effectiveness to quickly correct and help players make the shift from the uncontrollables to the controllables.

By the second week of the season, Daniel wanted not just to test the leaders, but empower them to step up. He devised a plan in which every coach would be "stuck" in a meeting with the league, and they would all be late to practice. He sent a text to the team apologizing for their delay and asked the leadership group to run the practice. They knew what to do since the practice plan was already posted on the locker room door.

As Daniel and the coaching staff walked in, a smile came across their faces. While it was not perfect, the team was practicing and practicing hard. The gym was full of energy. He called the team together and said, "I'm very proud of everyone who stepped up to lead today and proud of all of you who followed. The Washington Prep Warriors basketball team is *our* team, not *my* team. I'm going to pass on more and more responsibility to you as the season progresses. I trust and believe that soon enough, you will become such a well-oiled machine that you will not even need me."

Every Sunday, the team would complete a character activity, listen to a guest speaker, and eat a family dinner together. Afterward, the leadership group—Kevin, Eddie, and Archie—met with the coaching staff to get their feedback on the week and to include them in the planning for the upcoming week. In that meeting, the coaches treated them as equals, and over time they listened more and more to their perspectives and takes on everything related to strategy and culture.

As the season progressed, they continued to *pass the ball*, as one of the New Zealand All Blacks' mantras suggested. Not only were they running the warm-ups by the third week, but they also implemented changes in the process to make it more effective. In the fourth week, they took full responsibility for the checklist of the chores. In week five, they started practice and the post-practice team meetings themselves—leading the reading, journaling, and after-action reviews.

Daniel was working to create a team of followers *and* a team of leaders. He gave them the freedom to make changes in the practice plan, and even had them design a practice and make adjustments to practice times if they felt they needed more or less work.

After weeks of this passing of leadership, it took hold within the team. The team had to deal with Eddie, Archie, and Kevin when they got sloppy, if attitudes flared up, or when players weren't following through on their commitments.

But their success was most evident in the after-action review, in which the whole team participated after completing their individual success logs. Creating an environment where everyone felt safe to speak up was not easy, and at first, it failed miserably.

At the first practice, Daniel asked three questions, "What happened in today's practice? Why did it happen? How can we improve on weaknesses and sustain strengths?" Players only felt safe enough to point out the good, so Daniel asked, "Were we perfect? Did nothing bad happen in practice today?" The room fell silent. After poking and prodding, a few players mentioned areas to work on, but it was obvious they were nervous.

Daniel decided to employ a little trick at the next practice. He asked Archie and the lone freshmen, Dennis, to point out a negative aspect of the coaches. "Find something! Anything. Find a way to say it respectfully, but we need you to speak up on something that you felt was not beneficial."

As the after-action review started, Archie spoke up right away. "The new shooting drill we did at the start of practice was really bad."

"Why did it go poorly?" Coach Fred asked.

"Coach Daniel didn't explain it well, so we didn't know what to do, which made us try to figure it out instead of going hard."

Daniel asked, "What can I do better next time?"

"Let us walk through it before we start; that would be helpful."

"Fantastic, Archie. I really appreciate and need more feedback like that."

Before Dennis even had a chance to speak up, more and more players pointed out areas in which they had gone wrong as a team and offered some helpful solutions. People felt safer once they spoke in a way that judged the action, not the person. By the end of the season, the players were doing nearly the entire after-action review themselves; the coaches were the ones taking notes!

For years, Fred and Daniel had complained about the new generation's entitlement. Daniel finally realized these kids were not any different from previous generations, so it must be the culture that created the sense of entitlement.

It was hard to teach someone to be grateful when they were raised in a home that didn't stress it. It was awkward to teach a kid to say thank you to a coach. But Daniel had read that Gregg Popovich of the San Antonio Spurs always said to his players, "Thank you for allowing me to coach you." So as often as he could, Daniel let his players know he appreciated them, even though it seemed kind of crazy, since he was the one sacrificing so much to pour into their lives and serve them!

Another way they worked to build gratitude was in team meetings at the end of practices. Once a week, Daniel would ask a player, "Do you know any player or coach who really gave extra effort today or just had a positive impact on you?" The player chosen would get a Gatorade, a protein bar, or some other reward. While it was a small extrinsic reward, it was intrinsically rewarding and positive for the culture to have someone acknowledge someone else.

Thankful Thursdays became all about everyone sharing three new things in their lives they were thankful for. It also helped players stop taking the good things in their lives for granted.

Serving Saturdays was one of the team's favorite days. Once a month, they would invite kids from the local middle schools to train with the team.

Players would design their own workouts and complete the workouts while coaching a small group of young people. Not only did they get the opportunity to serve others, but they got their workout in, as well as the incredible experience of teaching a skill.

One Saturday a month, the team would perform a community service project, working directly with people in the community who were in need. Working with the disabled, sick, elderly, and poor helped boost the school's relationship with the community, while also helping the players become more grateful for what they had in their lives.

Daniel felt confident that each of these steps would create a strong bond throughout his team. It would also build a positive culture, one where players could grow, and the team could develop a strong synergy that would hopefully translate to an exciting and successful season. One step at a time, he kept telling himself. Daniel couldn't help but get excited at the prospect of putting this team on the court to see what they could accomplish together.

PART IV
SUSTAINING GROWTH AND SUCCESS

Calling up is not easy. In fact, it takes less effort to call people out because it doesn't require vulnerability, self-awareness, or retraining our default mode of operation. However, calling up brings new levels of satisfaction and fulfillment as we form a transformational culture. This is good news because it takes a great deal of emotional and physical energy to maintain high standards and sustain a special culture.

One reason the last section was so critical to the foundation of lasting success is that the people you select will largely impact the levels of stress and confrontation you will face later as you work to sustain growth and success.

The final part of this book focuses on the process of sustaining the growth and early success Daniel had in building that culture. In my own experience, I expected to find results as soon as I committed to the process and built the culture. How wrong I was! The hardest part in this process is that there are no guarantees. Only effort and hope.

As a society, we glorify really successful coaches and organizations (such as the San Antonio Spurs, the New England Patriots, the New Zealand All Blacks, and the Navy SEALs) who have built an amazing culture and achieved a great deal along the way. But the truth is there are many great cultures that are not in the spotlight and not winning championships. I do not believe that a state title, a national championship, or a world title validates a program or its culture.

CHAPTER 28

FOCUS ON THE PROCESS

The team had made it through its pre-season, and it was game time. Prior to their first game, Daniel sat in his office with his journal. In just a few moments, Daniel would emerge from his office and speak to the team one final time before they took the court for warm-ups. He had butterflies in his stomach, as if it were his first game ever. The last three weeks had been the most rewarding of his coaching career, but he was starting to unravel. Was it all for nothing? Would the team perform? As much as he had fallen in love with the process, he still felt like he had to prove himself to everyone around him. Not only did his pride depend on it, but his job and ability to support his family as well.

Daniel could immediately feel the tension in the air when he stepped into the locker room. Briarcrest Academy—the team they were playing—didn't have a good reputation as a program. Washington Prep needed to win this game big if they were going to be good enough to beat the better teams in the area. This was a tune-up of sorts, but one that would gauge their off-season progress in Daniel's mind. Daniel walked to the dry-erase board covered in writing at the front of the room to start his routine pre-game talk.

He walked through the four points of emphasis, discussed at length Briarcrest's strengths and weaknesses, their personnel, and the match-ups they'd soon face. Daniel then wrote a quote on the board: "Love the process, and the process will love you back." He talked to the team about how hard they had worked for this moment, then reminded them to go out and seize the opportunity! Daniel thought he gave a pretty good motivational speech. He then had them huddle together with their hands in the middle and shout their team mission: "Love work, love play, love each other!"

As they left the locker room to take the court, Daniel turned to Fred and said, "Boy, we better win this game big or my ass is grass!"

But the game couldn't have started any worse for the Warriors. Fouls plagued them, they made way too many turnovers, and missed tons of easy shots. Daniel tried his best to contain his anxiety and frustration, but with two minutes left in the first quarter and his team down fourteen-to-two, he called a time-out and proceeded to lose it in the huddle.

"Wake up! We haven't worked this hard for you all to come out here asleep tonight. Did none of you pay attention in the pre-game meeting? You all look horrible—lazy and selfish. Come on, you *have* to do better than this!"

But they didn't do better. Daniel felt like he was in a drunken rage the entire game—the players weren't listening, shots weren't falling, and the referees were making horrible calls. He paced the sideline like a caged tiger. With only three minutes left in the game, Daniel got a technical foul from the referee for pestering him on the sideline. The team made a final push in the last five minutes and cut the lead to four points, but they couldn't close the gap. The game ended, and they were once again on the losing end of things.

As Daniel walked off the court, his blood boiling, he passed by the referee in front of the scorer's table who had given him the technical. "Hey, ref! How about you don't screw me and my team every game this year!"

The referee was shocked that Daniel would say something after the game. But he was quick to react. He blew his whistle, called a technical, had the book record it, and let him know he had been ejected from the game—even after it was over. Daniel almost lunged at the referee, but Fred, Taylor, and Chad grabbed him, pulling him back. Once in the locker room, it hit Daniel what an idiot he had been. He would be suspended for the rest of the week, miss multiple games, and pay a five hundred dollar fine.

As he got into the locker room, he huddled the team together. But the feeling in the locker room was very different than it had been all pre-season. Players were unengaged, heads were hanging, and nobody wanted to share. After a few minutes, Daniel just said, "Fine! If you all don't want to get better, then just get out of here." And with that, everybody cleared out.

Daniel walked into his office and slammed the door behind him. He sat there at his desk, his hands over his face, trying to fully recall what had just occurred. Daniel knew he had blown it; he'd squandered his first shot at a winning season and a happy and engaged team. He felt like such a failure. He didn't know where to go or what to do, but he eventually found the courage to call John and ask if he could come over to chat. John was as cordial as ever and told him to meet him at his place in thirty minutes.

Embarrassed as ever, Daniel visited John after the game. John answered the door, and Daniel walked right into his living room and fell into the oversized armchair. "What a complete disaster! My team is so bad, and I was so blind to how bad we were. What a fool I am to think I could have turned it around."

With a stern look that Daniel had never seen before, John said, "There are no bad teams, just bad leaders. Now, are you here to mope or are you here to get better?"

Daniel was taken aback by the tone in John's voice. "Sorry, please tell me what you think."

"Well, let's listen to it," John instructed. He had Daniel record his voice throughout the game, from start to finish, so they could listen to it.

After only twenty minutes of Daniel's pre-game talk, John laughed and said, "Stop it there; no wonder your guys were asleep on the court. You put them to sleep before the game, droning on and on. As a player, did you enjoy listening to a coach talk for that long?"

Daniel, a little embarrassed, said, "No, not really. Actually, it was horrible, now that I think of it."

"Exactly! So be kind and keep it short. I said the same thing every game, no matter what: 'When it's over, I want your heads up. And there's only one way your heads can be up—that's to give it your best out there, everything you have.'[9] Daniel, I didn't diagram plays, scout opponents, or talk about our emphasis. If they hadn't learned it yet, they wouldn't learn it then."

As they kept listening, Daniel became red in the cheeks, embarrassed by the amount of yelling and how hard he was breathing. He could practically hear his heart beating through his chest on the audio recording. After listening to the first half, half-time, and a few minutes into the second half, John hadn't said a word. Finally, Daniel turned it off and said quietly, "I can't listen to it anymore. I'm so embarrassed."

John put his arm on Daniel's shoulder. "Peaks and valleys belong in the Alps, not in the temperament or the emotions of a leader. What if we had put a camera on you and recorded your body language? Would that have said anything different?"[10]

"No, not at all. Probably just would have shown a crazy idiot. I know I lost it. I don't know what came over me." Daniel's shoulders sagged as he continued, "I was so annoyed by my players' body language when things weren't going well. The referees missed calls because they were focused on the wrong things, and the parents in the stands wouldn't stop shouting at the team instead of just cheering them on. But I guess I did the same thing. My body language was out of control, my focus shifted completely to the uncontrollables, and I tried to control every player in the game from the sideline!"

"Can you be a process coach if you react emotionally to the result? How about your time-outs and half-time talks? Great leaders are good at listening. It's difficult to listen when you're talking the entire time, isn't it?"

"Yes, I definitely have to retrain my default mode of operation this season when it comes to the games and applying my coaching principles to

---

9   *Wooden on Leadership* by John Wooden
10   By John Wooden

our performance. I messed this up at the first smell of conflict. I'm totally ashamed that I was so fragile and unable to hold it together."

John smiled, acknowledging Daniel's thoughts. "Well don't tell me that ... tell that to your team."

Reflect and write: What message does your behavior send to your team members, colleagues, and the world around you about your values and focus?

Daniel knew he had to take ownership not just of his actions, but also the team's performance. He kept thinking of the Navy SEALs mantra: "There are no bad teams, just bad leaders." Before practice, he gathered the team in the locker room to take ownership, be vulnerable, and ask for their suggestions on how to move forward.

"Whose fault was yesterday's performance?" he asked the team. They looked around, nervous and unsure.

After a brief silence, Matt stood up. "It's on me. I couldn't make a shot, and the team counts on me to make those outside shots."

"Wrong," Daniel said. It was not on Matt.

Next, Kevin stood up. "I turned the ball over way too much and as a point guard, I can't let that happen."

"Wrong again," Daniel said.

And then, totally shocking Daniel and the rest of the staff, Archie stood up with his head hanging low. "Me. Our defense was horrible, and I'm supposed to be the best defender on this team. I didn't give a great effort at all."

"And wrong again!" Daniel said. "As proud as I am that all of you are trying to step up and take responsibility, you're all wrong. I'm to blame for yesterday. I'm the leader of this team, and it *starts with me*. I failed you all. We will rise and fall to the level of our leadership. I owe everyone here today an apology. I take responsibility for my actions and behavior last night; it was totally unacceptable. Also, I take responsibility for last night's poor performance; I failed to prepare you to play at your best. I hope you all can forgive me. I will not be coaching the next game this week due to my suspension. I'm really upset, but I'm working to see it as a great opportunity to help rethink the way this team and I approach games."

The players seemed to relax as Daniel spoke; it was apparent that they thought they might receive another lashing, but instead, they got an apology. Daniel then asked, "Why were we on edge, unsure of ourselves and nervous from start to finish of that game? I need your honest feedback, and to know what I need to do differently."

Dennis spoke up first. "I'm only a freshman, so I was just nervous, as it was my first varsity game ever!"

Kevin spoke up next. "I'm afraid to make mistakes, because I don't want to get pulled out of the game."

Eddie added, "I just feel so much pressure to be perfect. My parents want me to play in college, and I'm overwhelmed with the stress of proving myself."

"I knew we needed to win that game big," Matt said. "It's my senior season, and I don't want to lose a single game."

Archie, who was always one of the most honest and insightful team members, said, "There's too much talking before the game. It's really hard to pay attention or even think about remembering all the match-ups and emphasis—and no offense Coach, but your pre-game talks don't really fire me up. I'm ready to play as is, and it just seems to get me all distracted before I hit the court."

Daniel felt a lump in his throat. "Thank you, Archie, I really need that type of feedback. Does anybody agree with Archie?"

Heads nodded around the room as Matt spoke up. "No offense, Coach, but it is a bit much."

"I understand and I'm so appreciative of your honesty. As for your other concerns, I share in those. Obviously, I experienced a great deal of nervous energy and tension last night! I got caught up in the lie of perfectionism. Everyone talks about working to play the perfect game, but we will never be perfect. We should just strive to be better than we were the day before; that's all we can do."

Daniel looked to Eddie. "Perfectionism teaches us that what others think is more important than what we think or feel. It's all about proving ourselves, not improving ourselves. Kevin, when I react the way I did to the team's mistakes and the scoreboard, it's totally understandable that you would tense up and worry I might pull you from the game or even yell at you on the sideline. I wasn't helping to foster a growth mindset in any of you. As soon as I shifted my focus to winning the game, I became a results coach. I shifted my focus away from the controllables to the uncontrollables. If we want to be at our best, then I need to coach and you need to play. But that's not possible if we're focused on the results." Daniel looked at each of their faces. "We have to surrender the outcome. When we do that, we can rely on our training, not on chance. We can be our better selves and enjoy the moment. It's a paradox; surrendering the result actually gives us the best result. Surrendering control over the scoreboard gives us a greater chance of winning. Until we do that, we will always be our greatest enemy. Why did I struggle to surrender the result as a player? For the same reason I struggle now as a coach. I'm more focused on comparing than competing. I get caught up in the lie that my value as a person has something to do with my performance. I think that winning makes me better than someone else, because I'm comparing myself to them. Winning does not mean we are improving. Losing does not mean we *aren't* improving. When competing, I need to remember that whether I win or lose, it is about getting better as a coach, a leader, and a person. We must use competition in practice and in games to refine us, not define us. The great John Wooden used to say, 'Don't worry about being better than somebody else, but never cease trying to be the best you can be. You have control of that, not the other.'"

Daniel surveyed the room as he finished his speech. He watched as each player maintained steady eye contact and nodded his head as if to agree with Daniel's every word. He wasn't used to this type of engagement, but it was invigorating and exciting. While he felt he might have taken two steps back with his behavior at the last game, he knew his words and behavior moving forward would be proactive and not reactive. He could move his team to really buy in and win games if he just practiced what he preached. Daniel shook each of his players' hands as they left the locker room and personally apologized again for making a complete ass out of himself. He told himself he could do better, but he would have to wait almost an entire week to show his team just how much better.

CHAPTER 29

STRIVE FOR EXCELLENCE

aniel's words hit home with the players. And in a team meeting, they decided to implement some changes. So instead of going straight to practice, the team decided as a first step to redesign their locker room and meeting room. Their environment would have to match the attitude they wanted to maintain. The first wall was their competitors wall—at the top, in big bold letters, they wrote the phrase: "*Competere*: striving together for a common good." Underneath, they put the competitive cauldron rankings from practices. Around that wall, they put up other mantras and principles that would be essential to their competitive mindset, like "compete, don't compare."

They posted their team manifesto on the second wall, including their mission statement, core values, principles, and commitments. Here, they kept their checklists for various team responsibilities and procedures, as well as a schedule for the days, weeks, and season to come. This helped them to stay focused and take things one day at a time. The reminders were everywhere around them.

They decided the third locker room wall would be their tactical wall. They hung a large dry-erase board for diagramming plays and a bulletin board for posting statistical analytics, practice plans, and scouting reports.

Lastly, they left the fourth wall as a failure wall. At the top, they had a growth mindset statement: "Every event in life provides an opportunity to learn and grow." Underneath, they had a whiteboard with the phrase "The Voice of a Warrior" written on it. Just like in Google's early days as a company, players and coaches were encouraged to write down moments where they had fallen short. This would help to remind everyone it was a safe environment for them to fail.

Around the dry-erase board was an educational poster depicting the growth mindset versus a fixed mindset with various mantras to promote the former. This included statements like:

Failure is not fatal, but failure to change might be.

Failure is an action, not an identity.

Seek and thrive on challenges.

Failure is an opportunity.

Creating their own locker room was just one ritual to connect the team to their story. It caused them to reflect on, reinforce, and rekindle their team mission and values, helping them to actualize their goals so as not to be some pie-in-the-sky philosophy.

They started the next practice with a video session, but Daniel was not about to make the same mistakes he had made in the past. He decided he needed to engage them in reviewing the previous game. Each player took out his notebook and pen, and they watched five possessions from the game. Sometimes he would pick good possessions, and other times, bad ones. They wrote down the following as they watched:

1. What happened?
2. Why did it happen?
3. How can we improve weaknesses and existing strengths?

They then went back through and discussed each play. After they broke down plays together, Daniel picked five clips of something that went well. Sometimes it was the execution of a play, other times, a certain skill like a rebound. He would also lace in clips of college athletes correctly performing the skill or play. It was vital for them to watch things done the right way, as he knew it would help wrap the muscle memory around that skill.

Instead of putting together a scouting report, Daniel asked two players to watch one game each of their next opponent, and then put together a ten-minute presentation with some video clips. Instead of giving the scouting report of their opponent at the next practice himself, his players took the helm and educated their teammates about what was to come.

> **Reflect and write: Is your process of reviewing, evaluating, and studying your performance based on what your team members need or what you want?**

After the presentation, the players and coaches discussed the best strategy for playing that team then took to the practice court to work on executing that strategy.

It had been painful to sit out two games over the previous week, but it offered Daniel an opportunity to pass on leadership to the players and his assistants. In doing so, and reflecting with the staff, he learned that he could trust them with more in-game responsibility, as well as listening to them more.

As he approached the first game back from his suspension, he had a much different mindset for this game. He continuously told himself that he had done his best to prepare his team for the game, and he now needed to let go and surrender to the results. The last thing he wrote in his journal before stepping into the meeting with the players was a quote from the legendary NBA coach Phil Jackson: "The soul of success is surrendering to what is."

Daniel started the meeting with their traditional short mental routine of breathing, self-talk, and visualization of the game. Then Daniel went to the dry-erase board to draw. The players held their breath, wondering if they should buckle in for a long talk from Coach, but instead, Daniel just diagrammed where they should sit and stand during time-outs.

"It's important for you guys to be seated and everyone else to pack in close around me with your arms around each other. All eyes are on the center of the huddle. We want to create a very engaged team time-out, and this will help." Daniel turned to Kevin. "Instead of me babbling on, Kevin is going to speak to you before the game. Kevin, you ready?"

"You know it, Coach!" And with that, Kevin stood up and delivered a talk he had prepared the night before, after Daniel had invited him to do so. The players were motivated, focused, and enjoyed themselves as they took the court that night.

As the game got going, the team started hot, but their opponent, Central Academy, came right back with a run of their own. As Daniel felt his blood pressure rise, he reached for the family photo in his pocket and held it, reminding himself: *control the controllables*. He knew that if they were to be successful, he would have to manage not just their energy, but his own. To do that, he would have to be intentional about his focus, and he surely had to direct his mind and thoughts. If he could do that, he could create positive emotions, which would dictate positive actions, empowering them to play their best. The family photo in his pocket was a personal symbol to remind him to stay the course.

The first time-out of the game was incredibly uncomfortable for Daniel. It was like nothing he had done before. Instead of huddling together with his coaching staff then coming into the time-out to give directions, he started asking questions. He *knew* they were getting killed on the offensive boards, but he also knew they were getting some good shots—they just weren't falling. But did the team know it?

Daniel asked, "What's happening out there?"

"They're making a run on us," said Matt.

Sweaty and out of breath, Archie said, "Giving up too many offensive rebounds."

"Can't make a shot," Kevin added.

Daniel nodded. "Why is this happening?"

"We aren't putting a body on every man," Archie said.

"They aren't bad shots," Kevin stated. "We seem nervous."

"What can we do?" Daniel asked.

Eddie asserted, "We need to assume every shot is going to be missed and remind each other to box out."

"We need to keep shooting," Matt added. "Those are the shots we want; they will fall. Trust the process."

Daniel smiled. "Great job, fellas. Next possession, let's run *41 Power* and see if we can't get an easy lay-up."

As the team took the court, the coaches looked at each other. Fred chuckled and said, "They made the exact suggestions I would have made!"

"Absolutely!" Taylor said. "Ownership—they are going to put more effort into it than they would have if we told them what they needed to do."

Later on, after half-time, Daniel laughed as he left the locker room. He said to his coaches, "I'm pretty sure that was the most motivational half-time speech I've ever given."

The truth was, it looked nothing like the typical half-time talk he had ever given or even seen. It definitely wouldn't be featured in any inspirational sports movie. When they got into the locker room, instead of having the players sit in one room while the coaches "talked it out," everyone just sat in a circle. There was no "rank." The team did a mini after-action review. He listened to the players and helped direct their thoughts to areas they needed to address. He encouraged them to set two actionable and controllable goals to start the second half.

Before they finished up, Daniel felt they had left one thing out. So, he walked through it on the board—one play they had failed to execute correctly in the first half. As they finished up, Daniel noticed that nobody blamed one another, nobody was angry, and even though they were down ten points, they had all taken ownership, focused on the controllables, and bought into getting better in the second half.

As the team took the court in the second half, there was a confidence and an energy that Daniel hadn't seen in his team before. Instead of pacing up and down the sidelines, yelling, screaming, and trying to direct every action on the court, Daniel let the players speak up and play the game. The Warriors hit a few shots, quickly took the lead, and never looked back.

———

A month into the season, Daniel had players come to him about a lack of playing time. They shared similar sentiments:

"Why aren't I playing much?"

"What do I need to do to get more playing time?"

"What's my role on the team?"

Daniel had hoped he would avoid this challenge, but he realized that was unrealistic and unfair to expect. Just like employees want to get paid for their work, players expect to get time on the court for their efforts in practice. Still, he needed them to know there was only so much to go around.

The next practice, he asked every one of the twelve players to write down how many minutes out of thirty-two they thought they should play on average per game and turn it in on a piece of paper. He tallied the numbers and got a total of two hundred and eighty minutes.

"Well, fellas, unless we have about twenty overtimes every game, I don't have enough minutes to go around! There are only a hundred and sixty possible minutes to allot in a game, and you all are at two hundred and eighty. That means as a group, we have a disconnect from the reality of the situation. I take responsibility for this disconnect. First, I haven't communicated your roles or done my best to give you an opportunity to succeed. If that opportunity was clearly communicated and you realized you were failing to capitalize on it, then it would be clear to you why you weren't playing. Secondly, I haven't made those of you with less prominent roles feel valued. I struggle to empathize with sitting on the bench, because that was rarely my experience as a player. I need to do a better job and so do the players who play for more minutes."

To bridge the gap, each week thereafter, Daniel would meet one-on-one with each player to discuss how he could best contribute to the team within the game. Players would then write down commitments that aligned with their own goals and success to help the team perform its best. In the weekly coaches' meeting, they would discuss each player and how they could maximize their value to the team, with the understanding that—often—players were like sundials in the shade. If they weren't working, it wasn't because they were broken, but because they were in the wrong spot.

Still, as Daniel continued to make these changes and improve the team's process, he was struggling to enjoy the meaningful results of these changes. It almost felt like he was pushing a boulder uphill: it was only a matter of time before he got crushed.

CHAPTER 30
EMBRACE FEEDBACK

As the season progressed and the weeks went by, Daniel saw more and more instances of complacency. He didn't feel as if they were continuously raising the bar, or even maintaining the status quo. Players worked hard and maintained a good attitude, but they seemed to have plateaued in their development and growth. While he understood the importance of repetition and routine, he knew they still had a lot of room for growth.

Typically, this was the part of the season in which they would have some big meeting where Daniel would give them an ultimatum to get their act together—or else. But instead of lecturing, Daniel decided to listen. Instead of instituting new rules and expectations, Daniel wanted to brainstorm how they could snap out of this funk and get their act together again. One Sunday, Daniel brought the team together. They walked into the locker room, where Daniel had already written three questions on the chalkboard hanging on one of the walls. The players saw the following:

1. What is one thing we need to keep doing?
2. What is one thing we need to stop doing?
3. What is one thing we need to start doing?

The coaches then broke up the team into small groups of four players. Usually, Daniel would choose a member to lead the group, but this time he created a separate leadership group. He also created one group made up of the quietest guys on the team. He did so to encourage them to have more of a voice.

Daniel then addressed the team. "*Kaizen!* The Japanese word for improvement. In their business culture, it refers to the activities of continuous improvement that all members of an organization take part in. Toyota has been Japan's model company of *kaizen* for decades and has had one of the greatest reputations for having reliable and affordable cars. Anybody can stop the production process if they spot a problem. While stopping and starting the process seems incredibly inefficient, it's about refining and slowly improving the process until it runs without flaws. Anybody ever heard of Dave Brailsford?"

Daniel looked around the room and smiled. "Well, Dave took over the British Cycling Team in 2010. Typically, people come in and take over a program with big goals like winning the Tour de France, but instead, Dave had a different winner's philosophy—marginal gains. Look for one percent improvements. In just three years, he led Britain to win the Tour de France! Deliberate practice—which is required on the path to mastery—requires that you identify small elements of your performance and work on them intently. I argue that you should identify small elements of your process and improve those as well. I'm asking you to think of anything—and I mean anything—we can do to improve our process. I'm also asking if there's anything we need to stop doing so we can work to meet our goals. *We* might be holding ourselves back just by doing the same thing over and over again!"

And with that, they started to brainstorm in small groups. After each group had met for some time, they gathered as a team and discussed the ideas. Would they be beneficial? Would they be sustainable? If so, they decided to implement them. Daniel planned to ask these questions every Sunday at their team meeting.

For years, he had struggled in one-on-one meetings with players. He tried to figure out why this was the case. His best guess was that he had come up with more excuses than solutions for all those years. He could play each and every excuse in his mind. It felt like a broken record. He'd hear things like:

The age difference makes it impossible for us to relate.

They don't want to talk to someone who's hard on them and holds them to high standards.

They are self-absorbed.

They don't want to listen.

All excuses, but no solutions. Now, he understood relationships better and knew the young men wanted to be cared about off the court and on. He knew that if he wanted to engage his players, he would have to invest serious time and energy into listening and understanding their lives. So he went to his social worker wife, Brownie, for help.

Reflect and write: What are some commitments you can make to help bring more meaning into your conversations with others and to help grow and nurture those relationships?

"I know I need to be vulnerable, but after that, what do I do?" Daniel asked his wife.

"Ask great questions and then listen."

"But what if they don't say anything?"

"You love to talk a lot; we both know that!" She smiled. "But you need to be able to embrace the silence. Eventually, they will talk."

"What type of questions should I ask?"

"Well, I see a lot of supervisors and managers ask questions to help promote their agenda, but we need to focus on learning the other person's agenda and then discovering how we can support them. When you ask great questions, you will learn that some of your beliefs about them were wrong. The questions need to be about serving them, not yourself."

Daniel grew frustrated, but also knew she was right. He did love to talk and often found himself struggling to listen, especially to the complaints of his players. "What do I do when they are just negative and complaining? Especially about the things I can't change?"

"Sometimes, they just want to be heard. They don't need or expect you to fix the problem; they just want to unload it. Instead of asking them what they want you to do, ask them, 'What's next? What's the next step in moving toward a solution?'"

So, Daniel crafted questions that he could ask in each meeting. He trained himself to be a question man instead of an answer man. When they would complain or vent, instead of offering a solution, he would work on just listening and connecting with them. As often as possible, he tried to get them out of the normal meeting environment of the gym, locker room, or office, and instead, tried to talk to them over lunch or while walking around the school.

Before every meeting, Daniel would write down certain principles, mantras, and behaviors to help promote more productive time together. Things that came to mind included: eye contact, lean in, vulnerability, empathy, listen, and right questions are greater than right answers.

Finally, to empower each player to offer feedback and get things off their chests, Daniel thought it would be a good idea for each player to commit to meeting with Coach D for at least five minutes once a week. Daniel was set on making the most of these meetings. He was sure to take great notes after each meeting, so he could remember what to follow up on in the next meeting. *Baby steps*, he thought to himself. He knew he couldn't transform his team overnight, but he looked at it like hiking Clearview Mountain. One step at a time, and he would eventually get to the top. Easier said than done, but Daniel knew he had to shake things up and embrace feedback in order to deepen their relationships.

CHAPTER 31

EMBRACE THE STRUGGLE

The team had struggled to win many of their games during the early part of the season. They had an abysmal four-to-eight record going into the Christmas break. While the players and coaches were still upbeat and focused on the process, the losses were taking their toll. While Daniel and his athletic director, Bill, were cleaning up the gym after yet another loss, Daniel confided one of his fears to Bill.

"We have stayed positive so far, but the next six games on our schedule are some of the hardest. I think I made a grave mistake in creating this difficult of a schedule for these boys."

Bill replied, "I get that same feeling, but I also know that you fail them if you don't let them fail. They need these obstacles and challenges in their path."

Daniel replied, "But this might be too crushing of a blow to their self-esteem for them to recover from."

Bill shook his head. "You aren't destroying their self-esteem. Just the opposite. Continue to believe in them as they work hard through these temporary failures, and it will build character when they triumph in the experience. Great leaders don't remove painful experiences, but they support their people through them. You're pushing them and yourself way outside of your comfort zone. In return, you are giving them an incredible opportunity to grow as players, as people, and as a team."

Daniel nodded. "I guess I just sometimes wonder if it is worth the struggle."

"A rather wise and precocious man once said, 'Who you are is defined by what you are willing to struggle for.'[11] Don't forget that over the course of the next month."

———

The next game was a blowout of the worst kind. The Warriors played their rivals, who happened to be the top-ranked team in the state. Still, it was not the scoreboard or the opponent that left Daniel in such a rage. It was the lack of effort and fight—the biggest loss in his coaching career. He had kept his cool through every time-out and even at half-time, but he now felt like he was about to lose his cool completely.

As he walked to the locker room with his staff, they could all sense he was about to lose it. Daniel barked out, "I've never been so embarrassed. I've been so understanding throughout the season, and I've done my very best. I don't know how I'm supposed to take ownership of this team's lack of effort right now! I think they might need an old-school chewing-out."

The coaches looked at each other. Chad was the first to speak up. "Daniel, is that what the team needs right now? Or is that just what you want?"

Daniel grew red in the face. He was embarrassed, but unable to admit it. He stormed into the locker room. "Everyone, huddle up!" Daniel shouted, and the team quickly formed a circle. You could feel a tension that hadn't been in the room since it appeared during the first game of the season.

Daniel looked every one of them in the eyes and took a deep breath as he thought: *See the person. Lead with love. Act by principles, not feelings.* After what seemed like minutes, Daniel quietly said to the team, "I just want you to know that I love every one of you." And with that, they broke from the huddle, quietly calling out their team mission.

As soon as they got to the car, they might get an earful from their parents. They would be criticized and made fun of by the fans and their friends. But Daniel had made the conscious choice that what those boys

11   *The Subtle Art of Not Giving a F*ck: A Counterintuitive Approach to Living a Good Life* by Mark Manson

needed more than anything else was for him to love them, regardless of their performance.

Tomorrow, he could do an after-action review when he was calm, but right now, he was just not emotionally ready.

It was Toughness Tuesday, and players started to share some of their personal struggles in the post-practice team meeting. It became immediately apparent that everyone was going through something similar. Parents, girlfriends, friends, and fans were relentlessly criticizing their performance and the team. Daniel grew incredibly concerned and could sense conflict within the players. So he asked, "Do you think they are right about us?"

Kevin spoke up. "Absolutely not. I have been on so many teams before this that have won, but people didn't care about each other or have each other's back. I wouldn't want to play with a different group of guys, even if we aren't getting the wins as we planned. There is something much more rewarding going on here."

Archie added, "I thought you were going to kill us after the blowout game, but you didn't. Typically, people would go away from that kind of game blaming each other, but no one on this team did. We just owned it together and decided to keep moving forward."

Daniel smiled. "I feel the same, fellas. I wouldn't trade any of you away. This is our team and I love every one of you, and I'm loving the process with you, but that doesn't make losing easy. Let's try not to forget that our self-worth isn't dependent on winning, scoring points, or trophies. Let's focus on our purpose. The more focused we are on serving each other, the greater the sacrifice we will be able to make, and the greater the challenges we will be able to overcome together."

Even though the losing streak continued, the coaches and players focused on those one percent improvements. They were improving. For example, they were losing games by much smaller margins, even against teams they had gotten blown out by earlier in the year. They'd lose in the last few seconds of the game or even in overtime. It wasn't a perfect out-come, but it was definitely a sign of improving.

As defeating as it was, most of the team could sense the growth and development, which made it even worse when Daniel got to work in the morning and saw Dennis and Eddie's grades. Both were failing one of their classes. Daniel responded to this unpleasant news by calling each of their teachers and asking about the situation. Sure enough, they had failed to turn in some of their work. They couldn't pull their grades up until the next quiz, which wasn't scheduled until the following week.

Daniel called John and asked if he could take him to lunch. He needed his help. At lunch, he told John about the situation, saying, "I don't know what to do!"

"What are you confused about?"

"Well, I could just ignore this little mistake and act like I never checked the grades and hope they pull it up. Or I could just give them another chance. I mean, how many more setbacks can this team handle? And it's not like anybody would know."

"*You* would know," John said bluntly.

"We don't have a hope of winning this weekend if those kids sit. If we lose this next game, we will be in last place in the conference."

"You shouldn't let the pressure of winning allow you to stray from your core principles. Otherwise, you didn't have any principles in the first place. You need courage and mental toughness to do what is right, regardless of the circumstances or potential consequences. Ralph Waldo Emerson once said, 'Nothing can bring you peace but the triumph of principles.' So that begs the question: Will you really sleep well at night if you stray now?"

"The possibility of losing my job and being unable to provide for my family is becoming more real every day. I have faced what feels like insur-mountable obstacles. And I haven't gotten the job done."

John looked deep into Daniel's eyes. "And you have made the right choice for nearly every one of them. Have courage to see these obstacles not as walls, but as hurdles—as opportunities to strengthen you."

When Eddie's father heard his son wouldn't be playing on Friday, he instantly called the athletic director and demanded a meeting the next day. When Bill called Daniel to tell him that Eddie's father wanted to meet—not just about the suspension, but about the mounting criticism of the poor job he was doing—he agreed. Fred and the other assistants advised him against it. "Are you crazy? No coach should have to endure that level of criticism."

Daniel could only respond by saying, "Criticism has two sides. If I want to grow as a coach, I'm going to have to listen to the other side—even if he screams, yells, and curses at me until he is blue in the face." But inside, Daniel didn't feel so sure. He talked about it with Brownie when he arrived at home that night. Daniel asked, "Am I an idiot for meeting this guy?"

Brownie smiled and laughed. "Well, you aren't the sharpest tool in the shed! But know that you are right to meet him. As hard as it is, we should work on not taking criticism personally. Listen to him. If you deserve it—change. If you don't deserve it—then you know he's the one with the problem, not you." Brownie's words left Daniel feeling calm, knowing he was making the right decision.

Daniel went into the meeting the next day with an open mind, ready to listen. Eddie's father went off on nearly every mistake Daniel had made during the season. Eddie's mother also attended, and she started to cry as she said, "I can't stand seeing my baby boy lose games like this; it means too much to him, and I hate to see him suffer."

Daniel knew Eddie was one of the most resilient and positive members on the team, and that he always found a way to enjoy himself, even during the hard times. So, after the parents had finished voicing their anger, he asked, "Has Eddie expressed any suffering or depression about this season?"

Both parents looked at him with blank stares on their faces. His mother eventually muttered, "Well, no, but *we* can't stand to see the team lose, so he must be way worse than we are."

"I understand *your* frustration. But Eddie has been incredibly resilient through all the trials and tribulations we have faced this season. Let me ask you this: What are your biggest concerns for Eddie over the next five years of his life?"

Once again, Eddie's parents were speechless. His father spoke up after a long silence. "Well, I guess I really want him to go to college. There are a lot of drugs and alcohol around that could distract him from doing that, and some irresponsible relationships with girls. And bad grades; I want him to give his best in school."

Daniel smiled and said, "Well, the good thing is that our team culture and this sport can help him avoid those dangers in life. And as painful and hard as these challenges are this season, they aren't as painful as they would be if Eddie learned them five or ten years from now. Let's continue to do our best to support Eddie."

As they kept fighting through the struggle, Daniel realized how struggles could have a special way of bringing people together, more so than the easy road might. The team was closer and loved one another more than any team he had ever had.

But Daniel could tell his team just wasn't all there as they started practice with three weeks left in the season. Mistake after mistake kept piling up. No matter how much they seemed to encourage each other, they couldn't get it right. Daniel blew the whistle and asked everyone to go to the locker room. "Get dressed! We are headed to dinner." Afterward, he took them to one of their favorite burger places in town.

Once they had finished eating, Daniel stood up. "I want you all to know that this isn't easy for me either. The road has been hard, and I'm afraid of losing my job. It's hard to admit that, but I'm afraid.

Reflect and write: Do you model the strength and courage to see challenges and failures as opportunities to learn and grow?

"Sometimes, I'm afraid I'm fooling myself, and we aren't getting better. We keep working and working, but that just isn't changing the outcome for us. Sometimes, I'm afraid it will be too late when we have our breakthrough. It's hard in this negative world to stay focused on growth. People are afraid of failure, but this is just giving us the opportunity to decide how bad we want it. Let's embrace it. This is our story. And the hardest times make for the greatest stories. Whether we break through as a team before the end of the season doesn't really matter. What really matters is that we are all growing into better men. When we face another huge challenge with school, our jobs, our relationships, or whatever, we'll have the grit to persevere. When we do experience success—we will have a strong enough foundation to support and sustain that success, because we will have been committed to the process the entire time. We will have the character to support where our talent takes us."

Taylor, the assistant coach, read a quote by Jacob Riis: "'When nothing seems to help, I go and look at a stonecutter hammering away at his rock, perhaps a hundred times, without as much as a crack showing in it. Yet at the hundred-and-first blow it will split in two, and I know it was not that blow that did it, but all that had gone before.'"

Daniel continued, "This is the mantra of the San Antonio Spurs and now the Washington Prep Warriors! Let's keep pounding the rock! Today, our practice stunk. We couldn't seem to do anything right. But even if we can't get anything right, let's use future bad practices as an opportunity to build character and give our best, no matter how poorly things are going."

Daniel watched as the team got up one-by-one to leave. He met each one at the door, gave them a big hug, and told them to keep pounding the rock.

CHAPTER 32

CELEBRATE ACHIEVEMENTS, PRAISE THE PROCESS

And just like the stonecutter hammering away at the rock, the Washington Prep Warriors had a breakthrough! The players finally seemed to accept their roles fully and played hard—real hard. To the fans and the parents, it appeared that they had magically come together. It all clicked for them, and they started to dominate their opponents and rattle off big win after big win. The Warriors won their last eight games of the regular season by an average margin of twenty points. Shooting percentages were at their highest, turnover percentages were at their lowest, and spirits were up all around.

They were still in last place as they entered the conference tournament, but that reality didn't faze them even the slightest. Daniel initially worried that winning might be a distraction from the process, but instead it just increased the joy and provided more energy to the team as they continued to *pound the rock*. Daniel significantly shortened their practice times, and instead focused on quality time together in order to build their culture and focus on steady, continued improvement.

The pressure was usually overwhelming in these do-or-die games. The conference tournament wasn't for the faint of heart. One bad game and you were sent packing. But Daniel maintained a steady attitude and decided not to make any big changes, but to approach these games as they would any other. In the first game of the tournament, they faced off against a team they had split games with during the regular season. While they had soundly beaten this team a few weeks beforehand, they struggled to pull away until the fourth quarter.

The Westlake High Indians were up next, and the Warriors had lost their first game to them in a triple overtime thriller. But business continued as usual for the Warriors. Trust the process. Pound the rock. Westlake High came expecting a tough and hard-fought game. The Warriors came ready to compete. In the first four minutes, the Warriors jumped out to a fifteen-point lead. They'd never look back! Daniel focused each and every huddle on how to sustain success and improve on weaknesses. During half-time, he offered quick, honest, and direct communication. As the minutes of the game wound down, they were on top by forty points! The players and parents were going wild. They were headed to the conference championship!

As the team headed to the locker room, Daniel looked up at the smiling parents. He knew some of them had lost their faith and trust in him during the hard times that occurred often during the season, but that didn't matter now. He knew that sharing this experience with them would mean a lot to both them and the players. So, he walked into the stands and asked all the parents to join them in the locker room.

Daniel then walked into the locker room with the parents close behind. The team sat in a circle, and their jaws nearly dropped as the parents came in and stood around the boys.

"Fellas, I invited your parents to come and celebrate with us today. One of the challenges of coaching, parenting, and leadership is how we praise. While I'm excited for our big win today, and I plan to celebrate with you, I'm not proud of you because you won a game where we throw a rubber ball through an iron hoop. I'm proud of you because of the effort, attitude, gratitude, and respect you have shown your teammates and coaches not just tonight, but all season. That is what I'm proud of, and that is what I praise you for today. Great job, fellas!"

And with that, they started their after-action review. Even after a forty-point win, they were able to point out areas where they had struggled and identify ways to improve. As they did this, some of the parents' jaws nearly hit the floor at how articulate and assertive their sons were. They huddled up afterward, and even the parents got to put their hands in as they shouted their team mission: "Love work, love play, love each other!"

Reflect and write: When people achieve, do you praise the process or the result?

Daniel was the last to leave the locker room after the semi-final victory. He showered there then changed into some sweats he had kept in his gym bag. Before he left, he decided to walk back onto the court and take a few moments to enjoy the victory. As he made it to half court, he noticed a stray ball that was nestled in the corner of the gym. Daniel walked toward it, picked it up, and dribbled it to half court. He turned around and, almost in a full sprint, dribbled the ball to the elbow of the free-throw line and chucked up a shot. *Swish.*

Excited he hit his first shot of the night, he dribbled across court to the other elbow and shot the same jumper. *Swish.* Back and forth he went, dribbling, shooting, and rebounding. It felt like he was running back and forth for just a few minutes, but during a quick water break he realized he had been going for almost an hour. It was euphoric. He felt like a kid again, sort of like he wasn't the coach of the Warriors, but rather the point guard. Covered in sweat and satisfied he had burned off his remaining energy from the epic win, Daniel calmly placed the basketball right where he found it and left for his car.

Daniel picked up his cell phone and rang John on the way home. He detailed just how amazing his team had played and explained to John he felt like they were almost a team of destiny. John mostly listened but offered some parting words that Daniel wouldn't soon forget: "Trust the process and the journey will become the destination." Daniel wasn't sure what to make of that statement, but the more he thought about it, the more he realized what John was trying to tell him. Daniel thanked John for taking his call at a late hour, hung up the phone, and decided he would need another shower and a good night's sleep before he and his team would get back to work.

———

The Warriors had just three days to prepare for the conference championship, where they'd face the Copper High Knights, a team that had beaten them twice this season. The Knights had some of the best big men in the state. They were ranked third in the state and only had two losses all season long. The Warriors had lost to them by thirty-eight and twenty-two points in the previous two meetings. But that was a different Warrior basketball team, and those losses didn't seem to faze Washington Prep one bit.

Daniel called for a practice on the day after the semi-final game. He was excited to see his team couldn't be happier to reassemble and discuss the previous night's win. Even more satisfying was that each and every player gave a hundred and ten percent of their effort, even though Daniel expected them to be tired. If they were, it didn't show. The team couldn't have been more focused and determined to earn it on the court. The practice ran itself, and Daniel didn't have to blow his whistle or pull any of his players aside even once. Pound the rock. Love work. Focus on the small things. Don't quit. All effort, all the time. Play until the whistle blows. His team was ready, and the championship game couldn't come soon enough.

After three sleepless nights, it was game day. Daniel had empowered each of his players to be part of the game plan and carefully listened to their advice and feedback as he prepared for the Knights. Each player studied video recordings and compiled notes and a few clips in preparation for the big game. The whole team even discussed a strategy to shut the opposing team down. These kids wanted it just as much as Daniel did, and it was apparent from the moment they stepped on the court.

As the two teams warmed up, Daniel noticed just how confident the Copper High Knights were. Who could blame them? They had beaten the Warriors pretty good the last two times around. However, it was also clear during warm-ups that the Warriors believed the pre-game was just another opportunity to get better before tip-off. The Copper High Knights walked through their warm-ups, hot-dogging every minute of it. In stark contrast, the Washington Prep Warriors grinded and battled in their warm-ups while remaining completely focused. They were so intense that they were all dripping with sweat by the end. Daniel smiled and knew in his mind and his heart that his team was ready. Adversity had sharpened them, while their opponent had faced little of it all year.

The game was not even close! While the semi-final blowout was a shock to many fans, it would have been an understatement to say the performance against Copper High was also a total shocker. Copper High couldn't score until the last minute of the first quarter. The Warriors dominated nearly every facet of the game from the start, and Copper High froze up the second they realized they were behind and this was not the same team they had faced earlier in the year. They fought during their time-outs, and the whole gym could hear the coaches yelling at the team.

As the clock ran out, Daniel's eyes welled up in tears. Not because they had won the conference championship, but because of how amazing it was to have witnessed such a transformation in these young men and himself over the last year.

After all the celebrations and cutting the net down, Daniel huddled the team in the locker room, looked every one of them in the eyes, and said, "I love you guys. Thank you for allowing me to coach you this season. I'm forever grateful."

CHAPTER 33

TRUE SUCCESS

After winning the conference tournament, the Warriors qualified for the state tournament, which consisted of all the teams that advanced from their respective conferences. The team had just finished their last practice and meeting before the beginning of the first game. Daniel remained behind, making final preparations for the game tomorrow. He agreed to be home in time so he could have dinner with his family for the first time in a long time. He missed those family dinners, and they were a cherished part of his off-season. Regardless of the next game's outcome, Daniel was ready to spend some time with his wife and two children. It was well-earned.

After he packed up his things and headed to the door, his athletic director, Bill, walked into the meeting room.

"Oh, hey, Bill. I was just about to head out. What can I do for you?"

"Daniel, we need to talk," he said gravely.

"Well, this doesn't sound good."

Bill sat down at one of the meeting tables and motioned for Daniel to take a seat as well. "Daniel, I don't like bringing you news like this, especially when things have been going so well. I know it's the day before the game, but I think you have a right to know what's been going on internally. The principal and the board met last night, and they have decided that unless you make it to the state championship game, they aren't going to renew your contract. I know this stinks, and I don't agree with their decision, but it's out of my hands."

Daniel's face fell. He knew he was still on the hot seat, but he wrongly assumed the enormous amount of success they had recently achieved offered him some job security. He was obviously mistaken and couldn't quite believe what he had just heard. Even then, he held his head high. "Well, this has been a truly successful year, regardless of what the school decides and regardless of tomorrow's quarterfinal game. Maybe not by their standards, but by mine. I'm proud of who I have become this season and of the impact I've had on the lives of the young men whom I've been tasked with leading." And with that, Daniel walked out of the room. He wasn't angry, just sad that this was what the sporting culture had become.

———

Daniel awoke early the next morning, unable to sleep. He quietly slid out of bed and kissed Brownie before walking to the bathroom. After a quick shower, he threw on a suit and tie, his regular game day attire. He was strangely calm under the circumstances. He knew he had trusted the process and did everything he could do to build a strong and prepared team. He had grown so close to his team, and the hardest thing about losing his job would be telling those boys he wouldn't return the next season. They deserved much better than what the board was offering.

The next game against the Lakeview High Bulldogs was a battle, and as well as they had been playing the last few weeks, it had been a while since they were in a battle like that. As they went into the final minutes of the fourth quarter, the Warriors held onto a four-point lead, but they were in foul trouble and struggling to get rebounds against a significantly taller team.

Kevin picked up his fifth foul with under two minutes left. He was out for the game. Daniel called a time-out to gather the composure of his team and make the quick decision on who would replace him. Daniel turned to his assistants, knowing this was a critical decision: Who to play? Matt or

David? Matt was a great defender and always seemed to come up with big steals in big moments of the game. But should he approach it conservatively and go with David instead, who would do a great job of rebounding? The coaches were split down the middle.

Knowing he was running out of time, he looked at both young men, who looked back as if saying, *Trust me, Coach!* He knew both of them would give the team their best, and he was torn. "Matt! Let's go!" Daniel said. He then turned to the huddle. The team reminded each other of the importance of boxing out and good shot selection. The last thing Daniel said was, "Regardless of the outcome, remember: sportsmanship, and shake their hands. We can celebrate later."

Up two with only five seconds to go, the Bulldogs made a skip pass across the court. Matt, anticipating the pass, made a move to pick it off. The ball hung in the air. If he got it, he would have a wide-open lay-up on the other end and a four-point lead. If he missed it, their best player would have a wide-open three. It was the type of risk Daniel loved his players to take. They were clearly playing without fear.

The ball grazed Matt's fingers. Unable to even deflect the ball, it fell right into the shooter's hands, who was parked right on the three-point line. The shot went up—*swish.* The buzzer sounded as the shot gracefully bounced under the basket and came to rest.

The Lakeview Bulldogs stormed the court! Another buzzer-beater loss for the Warriors; they couldn't believe it. Every one of the players felt like crying, storming off the court, and burying their heads in their lockers. But then they saw Daniel, head up, walking in the direction of the other team. This reminded them of the importance of sportsmanship, even when they didn't feel like it. As soon as the Bulldogs finished their celebration, the Warriors congratulated all the players and headed to the locker room with their heads held high.

The locker room was dead quiet, but Daniel noticed how many of the players hugged one another, smiled, and exchanged high-fives. They were upset at the loss but satisfied with their effort. They supported one another and were there in time of need. In that moment, Daniel knew he had built a strong and loving team, and their next coach would be a very lucky guy.

———

The pain started to subside a few weeks later, when the team gathered for their annual end-of-season banquet. Daniel would typically dread the awkwardness of the event, because many of the parents had burned bridges with him at some stage of the season. He decided to forgive them instead of holding onto his anger. Daniel knew that anger could only poison his life. In fact, many of his relationships with the parents had grown stronger throughout the season.

As everyone ate, Daniel put on the team highlight video for them to watch. However, instead of just featuring great plays from the season, he had mixed in interviews with the players sharing their experiences, the principles they learned, and the ways they had grown throughout the year.

It was time for the virtue awards after dinner and the highlight video. Every member of the team had voted for the most caring, the hardest working, the most competitive, and the grittiest player. Members of the leadership team defined the value and shared how that individual had lived it throughout the season. Then, the coaches presented a leadership award, as well as some statistical awards for different categories.

Next, it was time to honor the seniors. The coaches called the seniors to the front of the room and asked their parents to join them. First, one of the coaches spoke about each senior and read short quotes and stories that their teammates had shared about them. Then, one of the parents spoke about the growth of her son, how proud she was, and how much she loved him. There wasn't one mention of basketball, just a focus on all the great qualities he possessed. Then they awarded each senior with a plaque that said, "A Man Built to Love Others." After they received their plaques, each senior expressed his love and gratitude for his parents, teammates, and coaches.

Daniel had barely spoken up until this point, a change from years past. This particular award banquet had predominantly featured the players, with some of the assistant coaches as well. Daniel wanted it to be player-centric and knew the parents would enjoy hearing their sons speak. Many of the players and parents shed tears in the last hour, and Daniel had prepared one last message for his program, knowing this would be the last time he would ever speak to them as the Washington Prep Warriors head basketball coach.

As he walked to the podium, the last five years seemed to run through his head. The long practices, off-season workouts, team camps, late nights, road trips, angry parents, heartbreaking losses, and exciting wins. It was all there right in front of him, and he felt proud of each and every accomplishment. He knew it would be very hard to hold back the tears, as he felt overwhelmed with emotion when he started to speak.

"Experience is what you get when you don't get what you want. These young men did not always win as much as they wanted. They didn't always get the playing time they wanted. They didn't always score as many points as they wanted. They didn't always have fun, and the road was not always *easy*. It is human to want the easy road. Nobody wants the road to be full of hardship, disappointments, and pain. I know that as a parent, I want my child to win, score, play, and have fun. But the reality is, the easy road does not make us stronger. The easy road does not provide valuable experience. The easy road does not lead young men to greatness. The easy road does not lead to the top of the mountain." Daniel paused, looking around the room. "In our pursuit of happiness, we can end up substituting pleasure. The problem with pleasure is that it's based on instant gratification. Pleasure is about what's easy. Pleasure is about how we feel. So instead, we strove to make this season more about fulfillment. Fulfillment is focused on others and involves going through some hard stuff. The true team experience is not about pleasure; it is about fulfillment. We weren't trying to lose all those games. We weren't trying to make the road hard. There are a lot of factors and reasons we struggled to win this season, some in our control and many outside of our control. Yet, we continued to grow because we chose to see every obstacle, setback, and trial that came our way as an opportunity to learn and grow. We trained our character and built our culture. Brick by brick. We could have worked more on shooting, ball handling, or X's and O's. But we chose to make developing character a priority. We shared our dreams and aspirations with each other. We shared our struggles inside and outside of school and basketball. We learned and worked to love each other and build the team around things that really mattered." Daniel could feel a tear run down his cheek. "I'm so proud of every one of these young men—not because they won a conference championship, but because they have grown in character and virtue. Winning, trophies, plaques . . . those came second. We put the things that really mattered first: love work, love play, love each other. Parents, thank you for allowing me to coach your sons. To my team, thank you for allowing me to lead you."

The banquet ended as it had begun, with the boys hugging one another, noticeably sad that the season had come to an abrupt end. Most of the players felt they had more work to do and weren't satisfied with losing in the first round of the state championship. They all thanked Daniel, offered handshakes and high-fives, and trickled out of the room with their parents, mentioning how eager they were for the next season.

Principal Richard asked him to stop by his office the next day before Daniel left school. Daniel felt pretty sure about what they'd cover in their meeting, but that still didn't prepare him for the feeling he had inside. As he took a seat inside the office, he could sense Richard's discomfort with the situation, even though he had done this many times before.

"Well, I won't waste our time, Daniel. I'm sorry to inform you that we will not be renewing your contract for the new year."

Daniel smiled and calmly asked, "Can I ask why you are not renewing my contract?"

Richard seemed to hesitate then responded, "The board and I believe it's best for the program if we go in a different direction. We appreciate all you have done for the program, but we think we need someone new at the helm to take it to another level." Daniel wasn't sure how to reply. He was upset and felt the school had completely mistreated him. Even so, he decided early on in this process that he would do everything he could to remain calm and loving, even in the face of adversity. While Daniel would have preferred to give the principal a piece of his mind, he responded with a great deal of composure: "I understand. Thanks for the opportunity."

As Daniel drove home, he remembered how he'd always thought he might cry if this day came—but he didn't. In fact, he felt some relief. Instead of going straight home, he stopped in to see his mentor and friend John, who was quick to give him a hug. Daniel related the past hour of his life, and John listened intently.

"Do you have any regrets?" John asked.

Daniel answered, "None. None at all. I've made some mistakes, but I wouldn't change things, because they helped me become who I am today. The road has not been easy; it has been incredibly challenging, in fact. But I needed those challenges; I needed to fail to get where I am today. As painful as this is, I know this experience is in my best interest. I will find the growth opportunity in this pain. It just might take some searching. If I'm being honest with you, part of me wants to understand why this is happening in my life!"

> **Reflect and write: Think of one of your greatest failures or setbacks in life. How did it shape you into the person you are today?**

John smiled and said, "You don't have control over what life throws at you, and you don't need clarity as to why it happened. You need clarity of your beliefs, and you need to choose to live by those beliefs."

Daniel nodded, stood up, and said, "I won't claim not to care what people will say or think about me. But I refuse to allow myself to be defined by what they think. As I move forward, I'm going to keep seeing every failure and challenge as something that will push me farther from where I am to where I want to be as a leader, coach, husband, and father. I know I'm far from perfect, but I'm not finished. But for now, I'm off to be with my wife and children, who need me more than anybody else!"

John stood up to give Daniel one last hug. "I'm proud of you!"

Daniel confidently responded, "And I'm so grateful for your mentorship, friendship, and most importantly, your love."

As Daniel walked home, he smiled from ear to ear. He was excited to share the good news that he'd be joining them for more family dinners.

AFTERWORD

While Daniel missed coaching and being around his team, he thoroughly enjoyed his newly inherited family time. He enjoyed dinner with his family each night and worked to play with his kids more and be more engaged in their school and extra-curricular activities. He instilled many of his newfound insights into his relationship with his kids, taking opportunity after opportunity to offer teaching moments. After a couple months' work, Daniel noticed his children were less reactionary, more loving toward others, and worked harder than ever to complete their homework and mandatory chores.

He hadn't searched to become a better parent and husband, but this experience over the past year certainly helped him to become just that. He would find himself laughing and sharing stories with Brownie, as they shared a bottle of wine on their porch. That was something he hadn't done since his college days. Daniel regularly shut off his phone and took his kids to the park, a movie, or just sat close by as they worked through their daily homework. Daniel even started a garden, a new hobby of his. He found that gardening was a welcomed therapeutic break; he lovingly plotted the seeds and took care of the young fruits and veggies.

Daniel would regularly visit with John, and their conversations turned from handling difficult situations with players to larger exchanges about life. They discussed love, engagement, death, and how to rectify

Daniel's feelings of inadequacy while he remained without a coaching job. But that passed as well, and Daniel fully embraced his new calling—stay-at-home dad. It wasn't his first job choice at the time, but he loved it nonetheless.

On one occasion, Daniel breached the subject of looking for a new coaching job. "You know, I really do love being at home and spending time with my family. I don't want to take anything away from that. But I was so excited to implement my new coaching style and really work with these kids in the off-season. There was so much potential for that team, even though we were losing a couple of great players to college. I had some exciting plans to help them develop and hone their skillsets during the off-season. Now I kind of feel like I have all these tools, but no one to use them on. I just want one more chance to see what I can do from day one. I almost love the idea of joining a new program and starting fresh."

John listened intently. "Daniel—as you know, everything happens for a reason. You lost your job so you could grow in a different way. I now watch you garden every day and see a noticeable difference in how you communicate with your family. It's really quite inspiring to watch. The lessons you learned, the skills you acquired—those are universal. They will help you on and off the court. And they have. You have moved from a coach with passion to a coach with a purpose. Coaching basketball is a passion of yours, not your purpose. Your purpose in life is to become the best you and to do what you can in the present to make the world a better place. If you're ready to start using your unique talents and passion for coaching to fulfill your purpose, then by all means go coach."

Daniel pondered John's statement. While he did enjoy his time off the court and with his family, he knew himself quite well. He'd always longed for the ability to coach a young group of kids and help them develop along the way. Maybe the time was right; maybe he was ready to start something new. He thanked John for his time, embraced the old man with a bear hug, and decided to chat with Brownie that evening.

Daniel was nervous. He hadn't gone on a job interview for a few years now. He didn't know what to expect and wasn't sure he even wanted the job in the first place. It was kind of ironic: his first job interview was with the team he ousted in the conference tournament—the Copper Knights. He didn't particularly like what he saw on the opposite side of the floor, but knew these kids had a ton of talent. But that wasn't enough, as Daniel had learned over the past year. Talent alone means very little. Success is so much more than being good at something. It takes work. Grit. Dedication. Humility.

But Brownie suggested Daniel start his search locally, especially because the kids were happy in school and she didn't want to uproot them for a new job. So he did. As he waited to be called in, he noticed an older tall man walk into the receptionist area. He immediately looked at Daniel, surveyed him, and said, "Daniel? Hi, I'm Joe Piazzo, the AD here. Thanks for finding some time to meet with us." Daniel shook his extended hand and followed him into his office, closing the door behind.

Joe motioned for Daniel to have a seat then sat across from him, intently looking him in the eyes. "I just took this program over. And my first job is to hire a new basketball coach. The board was quite disappointed with how last season ended, and I understand you are in part to blame for that."

Daniel smiled uncomfortably, unsure how to respond. "Well, as you know... just doing my job."

Joe smiled back. "Well, you did a good job at that. We crushed you guys twice during the regular season, and the entire team was shell-shocked by what occurred during the tourney game. You wiped the floor with us. Anyway, your name came up a couple times, since we couldn't figure out why Washington Prep let you go. Mind me asking why?"

This question made Daniel uncomfortable. He didn't want to blame anyone or throw his old school under the bus. "I screwed up. Early on, I wasn't a great leader and while I did turn things around in my last year, I guess we still experienced a difference in vision. But I still think very highly of those guys and wish them the best."

"That's great to hear. We think you're a great candidate for the job. You agreed to meet with us, so you obviously think so as well. The reason why I wanted to meet with you directly is probably not what you'd expect."

Confused, Daniel responded, "What do you mean?"

"Well, here's the deal. I'm not from around these parts. I was actually working at a school in Texas. I was an assistant athletic director for a D-II college out there. In fact, I was next in line once the current athletic director retired."

"So then why are you here?"

"Well . . . like you said: a difference of vision. The truth is that I didn't believe in the program, and I couldn't handle the kids and their families. It was a private college, and so many of the student athletes only cared about the athletic part of their titles. The administration demanded wins but offered no support nor any input from the very staff they hired to coach these kids. My sister-in-law lives around here, so I decided to take a vacation and check things out. This was about six months ago." Joe adjusted in his seat. "After dinner one night, one of her friends at the table suggested I step back and figure out what's important to me. I was conflicted, disengaged, and couldn't really find my purpose— my *why*. I was being a bit of a smart aleck and half-jokingly asked her how exactly I could do that. Without hesitation, she responded with two words: Clearview Mountain. I didn't know what she meant, other than that she was referring to a mountain. But she explained that climbing Clearview Mountain is a popular hike for people who need space to think and find their why. Hiking the mountain was actually a popular spiritual retreat for many Native American tribes centuries ago." Joe shook his head. "Pretty strange for a guy from Texas. We don't do that sort of thing out there. So anyway, I went along with it, mostly because I didn't have anything to do the next day. Well, I realized that Clearview Mountain is a hell of a mountain. I wasn't going to get up that monster on my own. Right when I was about to turn around and head home, I heard a voice behind me."

Daniel was shocked. He couldn't believe what he had just heard. Before Joe could get out one more word, he said to him, "Let me guess. You met James."

Joe lit up. "You know James? How do you know James?"

"Like you said . . . around here, we find our *why* climbing mountains."

MOVING FORWARD

The journey to *Calling Up* doesn't end with this book. To continue the conversation, you can review J. P.'s website at thriveonchallenge.com or email him directly at jpnerbun@thriveonchallenge.com. J. P. also offers a number of different touch points, including:

The Calling Up Guide for Leaders: Go to thriveonchallenge.com and subscribe. Not only can you download the short workbook guide for coaches which includes activities to help you on your journey, but you will also get a weekly newsletter with links to podcasts and articles to help you build your culture.

Mentorship Program: Need someone to walk with you as you move forward in your journey? Email me for details to set up an initial call.

Consulting Services: My consulting services are customized programs tailored to fit your athletic department, club, or team's unique context. I work with administrators, coaches, athletes, and parents to create a special culture.

Workshops for Teams, Coaches, and Parents: Presentation, discussion, and activities to address your obstacles, provide you with tools, and start practicing the implementation within your system.

Keynote Speaking: We don't need more motivation. We need a clearer purpose and a better process. J. P.'s keynotes offer just that. His authentic, vulnerable, and practical presentation helps audiences engage in the real meaning of *Calling Up*.

Coaching Culture Podcast: Short thirty-minute episodes helping coaches on their journeys to become transformational coaches!

Culture Builders Podcast: Short three-minute episodes giving coaches strategies, procedures, and behaviors to help them build their cultures.

Blog: Check out previous articles and subscribe for new articles at thriveonchallenge.com/blog.

ABOUT THE AUTHOR

J. P. Nerbun is a speaker, writer, culture coach, and mentor. Although he was a multi-sport athlete, basketball has always been his first love. He followed that passion to the University of South Carolina, where he won an NIT Championship in Madison Square Garden in 2006. After playing in college, J. P. moved to Ireland, where he got his teaching degree in Physical Education and Sports Science at the University of Limerick, one of the top universities in Europe for sports education.

He coached for over eleven years in Ireland, Lithuania, Tennessee, and Pennsylvania. During his time in Ireland, he coached over thirty teams in five years at a variety of levels. At the age of twenty-two, he coached a men's semi-professional basketball team in Ireland and went on to coach the Irish women's collegiate basketball team to the national championship. J. P. was also the head basketball coach for five years at Notre Dame High School in Chattanooga, Tennessee.

Thrown into head coaching positions at nearly every level imaginable, J. P. gained an incredible level of experience—the best of which being his many experiences with failure! Having worked with men and women at various levels and with diverse backgrounds across all sports, J. P. understands how to apply the principles and methods for building a transformational culture.

Unsure of how to serve and provide value for a time, J. P. started his own sports consulting business in 2017. He just knew he wanted to be a part of the solution to the current crisis in our sporting culture. Since founding Thrive on Challenge, J. P. has served coaches, athletes, and parents around the world at every level and in every sport you can name. Regardless of sport, level, or country, he is confident that all coaches need support. J. P. enjoys sharing the journey with them to help them become tremendous leaders and build remarkable cultures.

**Thank you for buying this book.
You have helped a family in need!**

**5% of the profits from this book will go to the
Family Independence Initiative.**

Imagine all families across America having access to every resource
and opportunity needed to achieve their goals and dreams.

At Family Independence Initiative, that is our vision.

We are a learning organization that trusts and invests in low-income
families so they can work individually and collectively to achieve prosperity. Using Family Independence Initiative's custom-built technology
platform, Up Together, families strengthen social networks, access cap-
ital, and support one another in achieving mobility. Together, we consistently demonstrate that families achieve collective prosperity when they
have choice, control and a sense of community.

Our state-of-the-art technology platform is used by our families nation-
wide; we have collected millions of data points that definitively point to
family success; and our traction with stakeholders in key sectors across the
country continues to grow. Our momentum is charging a movement and
changing the narrative about those living in poverty.

Join us.

www.fii.org

@fiinational

REFERENCES

Dweck, C. S. (2006). *Mindset: The New Psychology of Success.* New York: Random House.

Achor, S. (2013). *Before Happiness: The 5 Hidden Keys to Achieving Success, Spreading Happiness, and Sustaining Positive Change.* New York: Crown Business.

Arbinger Institute, The (2015). *Leadership and Self-Deception: Getting Out of the Box.* Oakland: Berrett-Koehler Publishers.

Austen, J. (1813). *Pride and Prejudice.* Whitehall: T. Egerton.

Batterson, M. (2016). *In a Pit with a Lion on a Snowy Day: How to Survive and Thrive When Opportunity Roars.* Colorado Springs: Multnomah.

Beilock, S. (2010). *Choke: What the Secrets of the Brain Reveal About Getting it Right When You Have To.* New York: Free Press.

Blehm, E. (2012). *Fearless: The Undaunted Courage and Ultimate Sacrifice of Navy SEAL Team SIX Operator Adam Brown.* Colorado Springs: WaterBrook Press.

Braun, A. (2014). *The Promise of a Pencil: How an Ordinary Person Can Create Extraordinary Change.* New York: Scribner.

Brown, B. (2012). *Daring Greatly: How the Courage to Be Vulnerable Transforms the Way We Live, Love, Parent, and Lead.* New York: Avery.

Carson, B. (1992). *Gifted Hands: The Ben Carson Story.* Grand Rapids: Zondervan.

Cloud, H. & Townsend, J. (1992). *Boundaries: When to Say Yes, How to Say No to Take Control of Your Life*. Grand Rapids: Zondervan.

Colvin, G. (2010). *Talent Is Overrated: What Really Separates World-Class Performers from Everybody Else*. New York: Portfolio.

Coyle, D. (2009). *The Talent Code: Greatness Isn't Born. It's Grown. Here's How*. New York: Bantam.

Coyle, D. (2018). *The Culture Code: The Secrets of Highly Successful Groups*. New York: Bantam.

DeVenzio, D. (2006). *Runnin' the Show: Basketball Leadership for Coaches and Players*. Austin: Bridgeway Books.

Dorrance, A. (2014). *Training Soccer Champions*. Echo Point Books & Media.

Duckworth, A. (2016). *Grit: The Power of Passion and Perseverance*. New York: Scribner.

Ehrmann, J. (2011). *InSideOut Coaching: How Sports Can Transform Lives*. New York: Simon & Schuster, Inc.

Elmore, T. (2014). *12 Huge Mistakes Parents Can Avoid: Leading Your Kids to Succeed in Life*. Eugene: Harvest House Publishers.

Frankl, V. E. (1959). *Man's Search for Meaning: An Introduction to Logotherapy*. Boston: Beacon Press.

Gilbert, J. (2016). *The Principle Circle*. Jamie Gilbert.

Gladwell, M. (2000). *The Tipping Point: How Little Things Can Make a Big Difference*. New York: Little, Brown.

Gladwell, M. (2013). *David and Goliath: Underdogs, Misfits, and the Art of Battling Giants*. New York: Little, Brown.

Godin, S. (2012). *The Icarus Deception: How High Will You Fly?* New York: Portfolio.

Gordon, J. (2007). *The Energy Bus: 10 Rules to Fuel Your Life, Work, and Team with Positive Energy*. Hoboken: Wiley.

Gordon, J. (2014). *The Carpenter: A Story About the Greatest Success Strategies of All*. Hoboken: Wiley.

Hillenbrand, L. (2010). *Unbroken: A Word War II Story of Survival, Resilience, and Redemption.* New York: Random House.

Isaacson, W. (2011). *Steve Jobs.* New York: Simon & Schuster, Inc. Jackson, P. & Arkush, M. (2004). *The Last Season: A Team in Search of Its Soul.* New York: Penguin Books.

Kerr, J. (2013). *Legacy.* London: Constable & Robinson.

Kimbro, D. (1992). *Think and Grow Rich: A Black Choice.* New York: Fawcett.

Kleon, A. (2012). *Steal Like an Artist: 10 Things Nobody Told You About Being Creative.* New York: Workman Publishing.

Kohn, A. (2005). *Unconditional Parenting: Moving from Rewards and Punishments to Love and Reason.* New York: Atria Books.

Lewis, M. (2003). *Moneyball: The Art of Winning an Unfair Game.* New York: W. W. Norton & Company.

Lloyd, C. (2017). *When Nobody Was Watching: My Hard-Fought Journey to the Top of the Soccer World.* New York: Mariner Books.

Loehr, J. (2012). *The Only Way to Win: How Building Character Drives Higher Achievement and Greater Fulfillment in Business and Life.* New York: Hachette Books.

Mack, G. (2002). *Mind Gym: An Athlete's Guide to Inner Excellence.* New York: McGraw-Hill Education.

Manson, M. (2016). *The Subtle Art of Not Giving a F*ck: A Counterintuitive Approach to Living a Good Life.* New York: HarperCollins Publishers.

Maraniss, D. (1999). *When Pride Still Mattered: A Life of Vince Lombardi.* New York: Simon & Schuster, Inc.

McCormick, B. (2014). *The 21st Century Basketball Practice: Modernizing the Basketball Practice to Develop the Global Player.* 180Shooter. com.

McCullough, D. (2005). *1776.* New York: Simon & Schuster, Inc.

McGuinness, J. (2016). *Until Victory Always: A Memoir.* Gill & Macmillan Ltd.

McKeown, G. (2014). *Essentialism: The Disciplined Pursuit of Less*. New York: Crown Business.

Medcalf, J. & Gilbert, J. (2015). *Burn Your Goals: The Counter Cultural Approach to Achieving Your Greatest Potential*. Lulu Publishing Services.

Medcalf, J. & Gilbert, J. (2017). *Transformational Leadership: Lots of People Talk About it, Not Many People Live it. It's Not Sexy, Soft, or Easy*. Amazon Digital Services, LLC.

Medcalf, J. (2015). *Chop Wood, Carry Water: How to Fall in Love with the Process of Becoming Great*. Lulu Publishing Services.

Medcalf, J. (2017). *Pound the Stone: 7 Lessons to Develop Grit on the Path to Mastery*. Train to Be Clutch.

Niven, D. (2014). *It's Not About the Shark: How to Solve Unsolvable Problems*. New York: St. Martin's Press.

Olson, J. (2005). *The Slight Edge: Secret to a Successful Life*. Success Books.Pausch, R. (2008). *The Last Lecture*. New York: Hyperion.

Pink, D. H. (2009). *Drive: The Surprising Truth About What Motivates Us*. New York: Riverhead Books.

Rendall, D. (2015). *The Freak Factor: Discovering Uniqueness by Flaunting Weakness*. Charleston: Advantage Media Group.

Richards, J. B. (2001). *How to Stop the Pain*. New Kensington: Whitaker House.

Sax, L. (2006). *Why Gender Matters: What Parents and Teachers Need to Know About the Emerging Science of Sex Differences*. New York: Harmony.

Selk, J. (2008). *10-Minute Toughness: The Mental Training Program for Winning Before the Game Begins*. New York: McGraw-Hill Education.

Sobel, A. (2012). *Power Questions: Build Relationships, Win New Business, and Influence Others*. Hoboken: Wiley.

Sobel, A. (2014). *Power Relationships: 26 Irrefutable Laws for Building Extraordinary Relationships*. Hoboken: Wiley.

St. John, W. (2009). *Outcasts United: An American Town, a Refugee Team, and One Woman's Quest to Make a Difference*. New York: Spiegel & Grau.

Thierfelder, B. (2013). *Less Than a Minute to Go: The Secret to World-Class Performance in Sport, Business, and Everyday Life*. Charlotte: Saint Benedict Press, LLC.

Tough, P. (2012). *How Children Succeed: Grit, Curiosity, and the Hidden Power of Character*. New York: Houghton Mifflin Harcourt.

Turak, A. (2015). *Business Secrets of the Trappist Monks: One CEO's Quest for Meaning and Authenticity*. New York: Columbia University Press.

Williams, R. & Crothers, T. (2009). *Hard Work: A Life On and Off the Court*. Chapel Hill: Algonquin Books.

Willink, J. (2015). *Extreme Ownership: How U.S. Navy SEALs Lead and Win*. New York: St. Martin's Press.

Wooden, J. & Jamison, S. (2005). *Wooden on Leadership: How to Create a Winning Organization*. New York: McGraw-Hill Education.

Wooden, J. (2003). *They Call Me Coach*. New York: McGraw-Hill Education.

CPSIA information can be obtained
at www.ICGtesting.com
Printed in the USA
BVHW031402060520
578927BV00015B/579